Bicycle Touring in the '90s

Bicycling Magazine's

Bicycle Touring in the '90s

By the Editors of *Bicycling* Magazine

 Rodale Press, Emmaus, Pennsylvania

Our Mission

We publish books that empower people's lives.

RODALE BOOKS

Cover photo: David R. Stoecklein

If you have any questions or comments concerning this book, please write:
    Rodale Press
    Book Readers' Service
    33 East Minor Street
    Emmaus, PA 18098

Library of Congress Cataloging-in-Publication Data

Bicycling magazine's bicycle touring in the '90s / by the editors of
    Bicycling magazine.
        p.   cm.
    ISBN 0-87596-154-1 : paperback
    1. Bicycle touring.   I. Bicycling magazine.   II. Title: Bicycle
    touring in the '90s.
    GV1044.B54   1993
    796.6'4—dc20   92–34608
                                          CIP

Distributed in the book trade by St. Martin's Press

2 4 6 8 10 9 7 5 3 1 paperback

CONTENTS

◼◻ INTRODUCTION

Not long ago, bicycle touring was at the fringe of cycling. You set out by strapping your tent and 40 pounds of gear onto a 10- or 15-speed bike and pedaling toward parts unknown (mostly because maps were so bad). Dinner, and maybe even lunch and breakfast, was a couple of peanut-butter sandwiches, smoothly spread with a cone wrench. And you loved it. You were traveling at your own pace, self-contained, able to experience the country like few others before or since.

If that's still your style, the world is your Jif jar. But for many recreational cyclists, particularly those with limited time for an active vacation, the 1990s herald a new way to travel by bike. Hundreds of commercial touring companies offer cycling trips to virtually any place in the world, attending to every detail while you ride unencumbered by day and relax in comfort at night.

Here is your introduction to this new style of touring. Included is a shopping guide to more than 200 companies and the destinations they serve. In addition, special sections bring you up to date on touring in Europe and provide the information necessary for the grandest of adventures, the U.S. transcontinental. No matter where you decide to ride, this book will prepare you for a safe and successful trek.

Ed Pavelka, Editor-at-Large
Bicycling Magazine

Part One

A NEW STYLE OF TOURING

1 CYCLING'S NEWEST INDUSTRY

Twenty years ago, people would have chortled if you referred to bicycle touring as an industry. In those days, a bike tour was a way to express individual freedom. Right on. It was a way to commune with nature. Far out. But a way for someone to make money? No way, man. At least not until 1972, when John Freidin started a company called Vermont Bicycle Touring (VBT).

The concept of charging a fee for a group bike vacation was no overnight success. Even a decade ago, VBT was the only major tour operator, and bike touring was maybe a $2 million-per-year business.

In the next ten years, though, the industry blossomed. By 1992 there were about a dozen large companies and more than 150 small ones. According to estimates, total annual revenues are $30 to $60 million.

How Touring Turned onto the Fast Track

Spurred by the fitness boom and the renewed popularity of adult cycling, tours attract an audience much wider than the hard-core "granola crowd" that characterized them in the early 1970s. It's estimated that 30,000 to 35,000 people took bike tour vacations in 1990. Women make up the majority of the clientele for many companies, and most customers don't even consider themselves cyclists. They're simply attracted to the idea of an active yet comfortable vacation.

By catering to this group, the industry has been on a fast track in recent years, with three companies—VBT, VCC Four Seasons Cycling (formerly Vermont Country Cyclers) and Backroads Bicycle Touring—emerging as the leaders in the domestic market. The Big Three combine for as much as 75 percent of total U.S. business, according to VCC spokesman Raymond Lemire.

VBT sold $5 million in bike tours during 1990, and VCC Four Seasons had total revenues of about $5.6 million. But Backroads may be the most successful of all. Since its mom-and-pop beginnings in Tom Hale's Oakland, California, basement in 1979, the company has turned into a $6 million business with two dozen custom trailers to haul gear. Their glossy annual catalog offers more than 500 trips of 2 to 17 days, starting from less than $200 to around $3,000.

In its first decade, Backroads grew an average of 62 percent a year. In fact, it helped the bike touring industry gain a national spotlight when *Inc.* magazine ranked Backroads as one of the 500 fastest-growing privately held companies in the United States. No other cycling-related company made the list.

What portion of all those millions is profit? Although the companies are privately owned and closely guard their financial data, Backroads disclosed to *Inc.* that its profit was 6 to 10 percent of sales in 1988. Hale now claims the actual profit is less than 5 percent, or about $300,000 in 1990.

Big Business Introduces Big City Ways

Large companies such as Backroads make their money through volume, spreading fixed costs such as support staff, vans and tour leaders' salaries over a large customer base. This is why, as the industry matures, it will be dominated even more by a handful of powerhouse companies. Already, recent developments signal the trend.

Buying out the little guys. Two major founders have sold to business people anxious to make a profit in a fast-growing market. Freidin sold VBT for a reported $1 million to former ski industry entrepreneur Bill Perry, and VCC's Bob Maynard sold to Travent Ltd., which is owned by the former president of the well-known sports marketing agency, ProServ. Since changing hands, both companies have grown quickly, expanding into new domestic markets by acquiring smaller operators already established there.

Shedding regional identification labels. Companies that had been strictly regional are going national, even in name. Like Allegheny Airlines (now USAir), expansion led Vermont Country Cyclers to shed its too-local moniker last summer in favor of a name with broader market appeal. VCC Four Seasons has a separate division—Travent International—to handle overseas tours.

Adding more and better services. As the big companies compete for customers, their services are going beyond the sag wagon. VBT and Backroads, for example, have each added an in-house travel agency to provide customers with flight reservations and other arrangements for their bike trips. And in 1988, Backroads began marketing its own line of road and mountain bikes that customers can either rent or buy.

Selling adventures, not just bike rides. Major operators can afford to offer more than just a bike ride. Some trips combine cycling with other outdoor activities such as sailing or hiking. Others focus on cultural and educational experiences. Backroads, for example, has augmented its offerings with a Puget Sound bike-and-kayak package.

Moving into the business. Bike touring's hottest growth market is overseas. Although this territory has for years been the province of specialized outfits, the major domestic tour operators have quickly moved in. International business already generates 20 to 30 percent of total revenue for VBT, VCC and Backroads, and all three continue to organize new overseas trips.

Introducing high-style marketing techniques. Already, some big company brochures resemble coffee table books. Backroads's edition won top honors at the American

Catalog Awards, where the judges included experts from L.L. Bean and Bloomingdale's.

The industry growth was achieved largely with unsophisticated marketing techniques—mainly brochures, classified ads in magazines and word-of-mouth advertising. In fact, tour operators say most of their business comes from repeat customers and recommendations. But late in 1990, the industry suffered its first downturn in years. VBT's customer count declined slightly, and the growth of other companies also stagnated. Hardest hit were weekend tours, especially in New England. Analysts blamed increased competition and the struggling economy.

Now you'll see a more aggressive, high-tech approach as the industry tries to expand its audience. Expect even slicker brochures, magazine display ads, direct-mail campaigns, travel agent tie-ins and other innovative marketing.

The reason is profit. The top tour operators say that they've just begun to tap the market. They see millions of active people as potential customers. And they're probably right. After all, it may have seemed unlikely 20 years ago, but these days nobody is smirking at the concept of a bike touring industry, except for a few big operators laughing all the way to the bank.

 2 HOW TO SHOP FOR A TOUR

Bruce Burgess, a bike tour planner in Middlebury, Vermont, recalls a photo of a quaint New England country store. Parked in front were three vans, each from a different tour company. Besides a laugh, the picture raises two questions you've probably asked if you've considered a commercial bike tour:

1   Are there real differences among tour companies?
2. How can I be sure to choose the right one?

The answer to the first question is yes. Although many tours cover the same routes (and country stores), there are plenty of differences. Some cost too much, some are bargains. Some are two-wheeled parties, others are slow processions. Some are for experienced cyclists, others for once-a-year riders. Which brings us to the second, even bigger question. Yes, you can discover a great cycling vacation suited to your ability, tastes and finances. All it takes is some comparison shopping.

To dramatize this, we compared two competing tours in California's popular wine country. Even if you're not interested in this particular area, the comparison will teach you how to shop for any tour. You'll learn how to ask the right questions and spot hidden costs, for instance. And you'll discover whether it makes more sense to forget the tour companies altogether and do the trip on your own.

Make a List of Hot Prospects

First, find out which companies service the area you're interested in. Check the guide at the back of this book. For an annually updated list of tour operators, send $5 to the League of American Wheelmen (LAW) Tourfinder, Suite 120, 190 W. Ostend St., Baltimore, MD 21230-3755. This list includes information on tour lengths, prices and accommodations.

Next, send for brochures. (For the wine country, the examples we've chosen are industry giant Backroads Bicycle Touring, and Bicycle Adventures, a midsize operator based in Olympia, Washington.) Read this literature closely and make a list of what's offered on each trip. Then call the companies and pepper them with questions. Record the answers in your own homemade chart so you can make direct comparisons of features that are important to you.

Analyze what you get for the price. Base prices can be deceiving. When comparing them don't just ask "How much?" but also "What's included?" For example, in describing its wine country trip, the Backroads brochure lists "hot-air balloon and glider rides for adventure." Bicycle Adventures cites "an early-morning hot-air balloon ride." Nowhere does either company mention that these optional side trips cost extra.

On international tours, the price of a bike rental and airport van shuttle are usually included in the base price. On most domestic trips, however, these costs are add-ons and may run more than $150.

But the airport shuttle doesn't always ensure convenience. In our example, each company's van makes only one daily pickup and delivery at San Francisco's airport. It's up to you to arrange your flight accordingly. For both companies, pickup is at noon, while at the end of the trip they deliver you in the evening. If the airline schedule can't accommodate these times, you may be forced to pay for other transportation or an extra night or two of lodging.

Study schedules for riding details. Tour company brochures are so crowded with postcard pictures and dreamy descriptions of inns and sumptuous meals, it's sometimes hard to find much about the purported reason for the trip: the riding.

When you call a company, ask for cycling specifics (types of roads, amount of traffic, terrain and so forth). If office personnel are unable to provide answers or direct you to someone who will, it's an indicator of an inexperienced or shoestring-budget operation—one that you may want to avoid. Backroads and Bicycle Adventures have people in their offices who have led trips and can answer these questions.

On many tours, the entire group covers the same route. If you're an experienced cyclist among novices, this can be extremely limiting. Ask if any provisions are made for those who want to do more than the prescribed daily mileage. In the wine country, for instance, both companies' basic route is a flat one through the valley. To experience the challenging foothills nearby, you need to diverge.

The two companies handle this in a slightly different manner. Bicycle Adventures gives tour leaders leeway to vary the route depending on the group's abilities and wishes. Beyond this, individuals are told of detours that can add extra mileage. Conversely, Backroads offers three or four daily route options, all with maps. On day four, for example, you can choose among rides of 45, 52 or 60 miles.

The routes are fairly similar and end at the same place, but only one includes sag support for every mile.

Differences in itinerary can also affect your decision. For instance, the Backroads tour visits five inns in five nights. The Bicycle Adventures trip stays at the same inn for two of the five nights, creating a "layover" day in which cycling is optional.

In any case, it's a good idea to plan your trip early. Ask the company about the best time of year to go. In the wine country, the harvest makes fall a favorite. But to ensure a spot, you need reservations six months in advance, rather than just two or three months as advised for other times of year.

Also ask about specialty tours. Both companies feature singles trips, and Backroads offers "health and fitness" tours, complete with nutritious menus and lectures on health and performance. It also has "art lovers'" tours that visit studios of local artists. With the boom in touring companies, you'll find more of them offering unusual trips to set themselves apart.

In addition, be sure to confirm your price when making a reservation. Some tours have seasonal variations, and prices of international tours are sometimes raised abruptly to keep up with exchange rates.

Scrutinize the meal plans. Don't assume that every meal is included in the base price. Some companies, especially on European tours, do not provide lunch, an arrangement that can be inconvenient and expensive for you. On most days in the wine country, Backroads and Bicycle Adventures provide full breakfasts, picnic lunches, snacks and gourmet dinners, but on some days you're on your own for one or two meals.

Another way companies lower their costs is by having a limited menu. On some tours, the entire group eats the same meals. In other cases, companies restrict your choice to two or three entrées. This can be disappointing, especially at fine inns and restaurants that offer so much more. Also, some companies will provide options for vegetarians and those with other dietary restrictions. Most do not pay for alcoholic beverages.

Look at lodging quality. Backroads and Bicycle Adventures generally use the same luxury lodging on their wine country trips. The difference is that Backroads includes the inns' names and descriptions in its brochure, while Bicycle Adventures doesn't. This is because it fears that publicity might ruin some of the little-known places and that potential customers might use the information to plan their own tours.

In any case, before you decide on a tour, learn as much as possible about the places where you'll stay. After all, this is where the bulk of your money goes. In addition to size, atmosphere and history, ask about location. Since you're without a car, it's advantageous to have attractions at the inn or within a short walk or bike ride.

Both Backroads and Bicycle Adventures guarantee a private bathroom each night, but many tour companies use small inns or bed-and-breakfasts with shared facilities. If this is important to you and it's not clear in the brochure, ask.

Learn about the leaders. A tour leader must be a cheerleader, mechanic, guide, psychologist, historian and friend. It's not easy, and when it's done poorly, you'll notice.

At some small companies, the owner is the only full-time leader. Others hire college students on summer break. Backroads and Bicycle Adventures employ experienced, full-time guides. New hires are paired with veteran leaders to ensure that no tour is led by two rookies.

At both companies, one tour leader drives the support van while the other cycles. One interesting difference is that the Backroads cycling guide stays at the back as a "sweep." At Bicycle Adventures, the leader moves among the riders and only drops back if someone doesn't arrive at a checkpoint when expected.

Another interesting variation is that every Backroads tour has both a female and male leader, the idea being that guests of both genders will feel more comfortable.

Critique the clientele. "We cater to all ages." Ask a few companies the average age of their customers and you're sure to hear this line. Unfortunately, this is a sales pitch, not an answer. Ending up in a group that's too old or too young is a major complaint among tour takers. Don't accept anything less than specific age averages.

While both companies in our example attract middle-aged professional people, Backroads groups are usually larger. In fact, it'll cancel a tour unless it has at least six participants. Conversely, Bicycle Adventures will run a trip even if only one person has signed up. In such cases, it does give the person a choice of transferring to another tour.

Ask about company policy in this regard and whether there is a chance the tour you're interested in might be canceled due to insufficient customers. If you can't change your schedule to accommodate such a development, look for another company with a firm commitment to the tour and date you want.

Read the fine print. When examining a brochure, be sure to turn to the fine print of the general information or policy section. Hidden costs lurk here.

For instance, within the Backroads brochure, in the middle of a thick paragraph entitled "Inns," this sentence appears: "If you sign up within 60 days of a trip (120 days for all trips outside North America) . . . and we are unable to match you with a roommate, the single supplement fee will apply." You have to call to discover that this charge is $255 for the wine country trip. By comparison, Bicycle Adventures assumes the financial onus for finding you a roommate, and if you end up in a single room without asking for it, there's no extra charge.

Other financial policies may be strict or liberal, too. For instance, let's say some emergency forces you to change your plans after you've registered. Bicycle Adventures allows you to transfer into a tour offered at another time. This can be done with no penalty until the last 30 days before your tour. From 15 to 29 days, it costs $25. Up to this time, you can apply your money to any trip the company offers in the subsequent 18 months. At Backroads, if you want to switch tours more than 60 days ahead of time, the cost is $50. During the last 60 days, transfer requests are treated as cancellations and no refunds are given unless the company is able to fill your space. Even if a substitute is found, you lose your $200 deposit. Such situations are treated on a case-by-case basis, though. For instance, the policy can be disregarded for deaths in the immediate family or if you're transferring from a popular tour to one that may not otherwise meet its minimum rider requirement. In addition, cancellation insurance is offered.

Check out the rental equipment. Even if you're taking your bike, you can learn a great deal about a company by the kind of bicycles it rents to its customer. For instance, a high-end rental usually means you're in for some good cycling. However, a fleet of old, Mary Poppins 3-speeds is a good indication that cycling is not the centerpiece of the trip. This is sometimes the case on overseas tours. If you're planning a trip to Europe, for instance, make sure to ask what type of bike is supplied and how old it is.

The companies in our example pass this test well. Bicycle Adventures uses Specialized, Klein, Trek, Claud Butler and Schwinn bikes with index shifting, a choice of saddles, a drop or flat handlebar, a seat bag and optional handlebar bag and a cyclecomputer. Each bike is overhauled annually.

Backroads has its own brand of road and mountain bikes, made by Fuji. These feature index shifting, a drop or flat handlebar, Kevlar-belted tires, a rearview mirror and a handlebar bag. Each bike is replaced after two years.

How to Judge Companies

Weigh the size and experience of the companies you're considering. Although experience is more important, size can play a role. For instance, many small companies use a crowded cargo van as a sag wagon. Should bad weather force more than a couple of riders inside, you may be in for a frustrating day. In addition, a large company such as Backroads offers more trip dates to choose from, a big, responsive office staff and a fleet of 21 custom-designed trailers equipped with kitchens and portable picnic tables. Bicycle Adventures features a passenger van and trailer, and a homey feel with its smaller groups. Depending on your preference, bigger may be better—or not.

But both companies have the same main thing: a history of successful tours. Make sure the companies you're considering do, too. Learn how long they have run the trip you're considering. You probably don't want to spend thousands of dollars to be a guinea pig. Ask for names of people who've done the tour. Certainly no company will refer you to a disgruntled customer, but at least the reference can answer your questions honestly with no stake in the company's future.

Is It Worth Doing Yourself?

If you don't mind mapping your route, finding and securing accommodations and carrying gear, you may want to plan your own trip instead of paying a tour company. This can be inexpensive, especially if you're not too particular about where you sleep. However, if you want to replicate the inn-to-inn experience of an organized tour, be prepared for some obstacles.

The biggest problem may be getting a room at the type of first-class inns the tour companies usually use. Tour operators book large blocks of rooms more than a year in advance, forcing you to make reservations at least 12 months before your trip. Even then, there's no guarantee you can string together the different inns on the nights you need them.

What's more, tour companies get a 40 to 60 percent discount off regular prices, according to a spokesperson for Sonoma Mission Inn, one of the stops on the Backroads tour. This is because of the high volume of business they bring. At the Sonoma Mission, an individual has to pay $195 to $295 per night, but Backroads may get rooms for half as much. Tour companies make their profits by charging a percentage markup over these discount rates.

When you plan a trip on your own, you get no discounts. You also forfeit the camaraderie, security and convenience of a commercial tour. But you do save money. For instance, in 1991 a couple had to pay $2,196 to take the basic Backroads wine country tour. But if they could have gotten reservations, the five inns on the trip would have all together cost $687 to $922.

Planning a trip takes work, though. To help, both Bikecentennial and LAW publish guides: "The Cyclists' Yellow

Pages" from Bikecentennial (Box 8308, Missoula, MT 59807; phone 406-721-1776) and "Bicycle USA Almanac" from LAW (Suite 120, 190 W. Ostend St., Baltimore, MD 21230-3755; phone 800-288-BIKE). Each includes state-by-state and foreign listings of touring information. They tell you where to write for local cycling maps and publications. They also include addresses and phone numbers of experienced local cyclists who can help you plan a good route. These guides are available to members only. Write for a membership form and information on the current annual fee.

General information is available free from state tourism boards. Local chambers of commerce can provide accommodation lists. As you might expect, the research is usually easier for domestic trips, but international planning isn't beyond reason.

▪3▪ LUXURY TOURS

George, a young professional from New Jersey, was adrift in an inner tube, sipping a beer.

Kevin, an electrical engineer from Boulder, Colorado, was learning to windsurf.

Ralph, a New York City banker, was tending the vodka tonics.

And Cara, a financial analyst from Staten Island, New York, was doing her nails.

It was a typical August evening on New England's Lake Champlain. The setting sun was just starting to rouge the sky, and the water in Kingsland Bay was slowly turning to glass. In the distance, you could see the Green Mountains of Vermont and New York's Adirondacks.

And they call this bicycle touring? Yes, but it was far from your typical trek. In fact, it was this group's second

---

The tour companies discussed in this chapter are for illustration only. Prices and policies that were in effect when it was written may have changed. Always check with a company for current information.

evening together and they had yet to ride. What's more, they were aboard a 77-foot windjammer schooner they had helped sail from Burlington, Vermont, that morning. Instead of tender seats and sore legs, they were nursing chapped lips and sunburned noses.

They were immersed in Vermont Bicycle Touring's (VBT's) Champlain Sail & Cycle, a five-day ($679) luxury adventure trip that represents the changing face of cycling vacations. The most popular VBT offering, it caters to discriminating outdoorsmen who prefer their exercise in varied but moderate doses and their food on china instead of tin.

Although billed as a cycling vacation, the trip featured just three days of riding. Depending on where the boat was anchored each morning, the guests were shuttled to either the Vermont or New York shore. There, they got bikes from a waiting van and embarked on routes ranging from 11 to 56 miles. You could ride more or less (or not at all) depending on your fitness level. The rest of the time was reserved for sailing, swimming, windsurfing, lounging and eating. The latter was about as good as it gets at sea. All meals were prepared and served on ship by a culinary artist named Sheila. Foods ranged from homemade chocolate-raspberry cake to an entire turkey.

What's Going on Here—Gentrification?

Bicycle touring was once a rigorous, spartan, even eccentric way to spend a vacation. The stereotypical image consisted of a solo rider, a bandanna wrapped around his brow, laboring across the country with bulging panniers. He slept beneath the stars and, more often than not, had his head in them as well.

But this has changed dramatically. Bicycle touring, like the sport in general, has become trendy in the 1990s. According to an informal survey of bicycle tour companies, the average client is an affluent, college-educated professional in his or her thirties or forties. Rather than an athlete, he or she is an active person with only a recreational interest in cycling.

"Bicycling has become an activity with a high profile and some social status," says John Freidin, who founded VBT in 1972. "It's the chic, fashionable thing to do. In the beginning it was almost the opposite of that. It was an alternative to those chic things."

Such widespread popularity has influenced tour operators in the design and packaging of their trips. Tom Hamilton of Butterfield & Robinson (B&R), a Canadian company specializing in "upper-class travel," says his organization first started using the word "luxury" in 1983 to sell its cycling vacations.

"If you bicycle through Europe by any means you'll have a great experience," he explains. "But there are a lot of people who would enjoy the experience but don't want to camp. They don't enjoy themselves unless they have certain comforts. By making this type of trip accessible and attractive to those who wouldn't normally consider it, you broaden its appeal."

Tuxedos and Champagne

One B&R catalog, which opens with a photograph of two tuxedoed gentlemen riding a tandem and sipping champagne, certainly plays up the posh. Among its most luxurious offerings is an eight-day ($2,095) tour of France's Loire Valley that includes deluxe chateau accommodations, gourmet meals and even a private dinner with a count and countess. Another offering is an eight-day ($2,200) tour of France's Champagne region. It includes private tastings at such famous cellars as Dom Perignon and Moet Chandon.

Not to be outdone, other bicycle tour companies have organized similar "deluxe" trips. Backroads Bicycle Touring, a California company that advertises in *Gourmet* magazine, has put together what it calls "the most luxurious bicycle-inn tour in America." A five-day ($798) excursion through the wine country of northern California, it includes nightly stops at deluxe inns and spas featuring everything from art-deco motifs to mud baths.

Besides its sail-and-cycle trip, VBT also has seven-day ($1,499) cruise-and-cycle tours of the Maine coast and New

England islands. Guests live the typical "Loveboat" life by night on a commercial cruise liner, then roll their bikes down the gangplank (if they're able) in a new port each morning.

Bill Perry, who purchased VBT from Freidin in 1986 and has since doubled the business, compares the bicycle touring business of today with the ski industry of the mid-1970s. "Early on you catered to the dyed-in-the-wool skier," he explains, "the person who would stay in a bunkroom as long as they could ski. Then slowly the market became more upscale. You began offering more amenities. The same thing is happening with bike touring. Years ago, it was a fraternity of dedicated, serious cyclists. Since they loved cycling, it didn't matter if four or six of them had to stay in one room. Now the market is bigger and broader so you need the good inns, the comfortable lodging."

Not Too Rigorous, Please

Like Perry, Ray Benton of Travent, Ltd., represents the new breed of bicycle tour operator. The former president of a sports marketing firm, he purchased Vermont Country Cyclers, Bicycle France and Chesapeake & Shenandoah Bicycle Touring and put them under the auspices of his new company. A novice cyclist, Benton was inspired to enter the bicycle touring business after taking the B&R Loire Valley trip.

"It was a marvelous experience," he said in 1990. "Now, the big challenge is to communicate the fact that bike vacations are an activity that can be enjoyed by a large percentage of the population—virtually anyone who has a minimum level of physical fitness. I don't like the phrase 'bike touring.' It sounds too rigorous. I prefer 'bicycle vacation.' In fact, I'm not selling cycling, I'm selling a lifestyle. I'm making a conscious effort to disassociate what we do from serious cycling. Once it's defined this way, it's going to explode."

Surprisingly, people don't seem to mind paying for extravagance. Tour operators say their most expensive trips are often the most popular. VBT's sail-and-cycle tour, for instance, is the first to sell out, and its cruise-and-cycle trip attracted 21 people for its maiden voyage. As the B&R catalog matter-of-factly states: "We dine sumptuously and pay dearly."

"Trips like this are a happening," said Al, a cabinetmaker from Arlington Heights, Illinois, and one of the sailor/cyclists. "You don't measure it in terms of money."

Potpourri Trips

While many companies are using deluxe accommodations and gourmet food to widen trip appeal, others are combining cycling with different types of activities and exercise for a more diverse experience.

There is a 5-day ($575) package from On the Loose Bicycle Adventure Vacations that combines cycling with whitewater rafting on California's American River, for instance. There's also an 8-day ($995) blending of mountain biking and skiing in the Swiss Alps, courtesy of Europeds, and a 33-day ($2,383) Asian excursion from World Expeditions that mixes cycling, river rafting, trekking and (are you ready for this?) elephant and camel riding. If you consider exotic experiences a luxury, this trip could be for you.

Among the less strenuous supplements are an 11-day ($1,590) biking and hot-air balloon trip across the Burgundy region of France from McBride's Earth Adventures, and a 7-day ($1,200) barging and biking trip along rural French canals from Rocky Mountain Cycle Tours.

Not only are such trips popular among "soft-core" cyclists, they're also the choice of many active couples with divergent interests. Kevin and Gina, for example, chose VBT's sail-and-cycle trip because it combined his love of cycling with her interest in sailing. For them, it was the perfect compromise.

"I once did a 24-day, 1,200-mile solo tour of New York State," said Kevin. "I'll admit getting up every morning and bicycling can get kind of old. I'm not a purist in that sense. This trip has been really different."

"Pampered Camping" Tours

Indeed, just as it's rare to see a new bicycle built along the classic touring design (most manufacturers have gone to the more popular sport touring models), no-frills loaded touring may one day be considered a vestige of the sport's crude past.

"I've seen a substantial decline in traditional touring during the last half of the 1980s," says Bud Reed of Vermont Bicycle Touring. "The baby boomers are now into high-tech jobs. They have plenty of money, a couple of kids and less time. Rather than spending ten days plodding along on a touring bike with camping equipment, they can cover the same distance on a commercial tour and stay in nice places and use their credit cards."

Bikecentennial, a national organization that maps bicycle routes and runs tours, has witnessed a marked shift in its market during the last few years. Although its cross-country route maps continue to sell well, executive director Gary MacFadden says Bikecentennial's own tours have become shorter, easier (van-supported) and more diverse in recent years.

Perhaps the most ironic example of this evolution is the popular "pampered camping" trips offered by Backroads Bicycle Touring. These backcountry getaways to a variety of areas include all the necessary gear, a guide to show you how it's used and a sag wagon to lug it to the next campsite. In addition, as the brochure describes, "the meals from our custom kitchen-on-wheels are fit for royalty." Such trips range in price from $159 to $1,527.

Expert Advice: How to Get the Tour You Really Want

Certainly, the trend toward luxury/adventure cycling trips will continue. Tour operators forecast steady growth in a slowly widening field. In fact, as the competition intensifies, expect to see some outlandish offerings in some exotic locales (beach cruising on Bora Bora, anyone?). But is this type of trip for you?

Chances are, if you're a racer or serious fitness rider, you'll be disappointed at the cycling ability of your fellow vacationers—and the daily mileage. Most tour leaders can easily design more challenging routes, however. But training is not what these trips were devised for. When your nose is on the handlebar, you're missing what you paid for—beautiful scenery, a refreshing atmosphere and the simple joy of exploring by bike.

For the beginning and intermediate cyclist, such trips are ideal. You'll not only learn about a new part of the world, you'll also become educated about your bicycle, your riding and the group dynamics of cycling with others. In the end, you'll probably have an even keener interest in the sport.

But before you put a deposit on that five-day bicycle/ mushing/hang-gliding tour of Greenland, consider that "adventure" and especially "luxury" are ill-defined, subjective terms.

According to tour operators, the best way to make sure you get what you pay for is to ask the company for referrals—a list of people you can call who've taken the trip before.

Reed of VBT also recommends dealing with a reputable and experienced company. But even then, you should examine the catalog carefully. "If you're going to Europe," he explains, "do they provide transportation from the airport to the first hotel? If not, how much does it cost? What type of bicycle is provided? A lot of gourmet trips don't focus as much on cycling as on accommodations and meals. In fact, the cycling portion can be pretty lacking. They simply turn you loose and say, 'See ya at the next hotel.' Make sure there's someone along to fix flats."

Perry advises prospective tourists to beware of luxury claims at budget prices. "Luxury is easy to say and not develop," he says. "Don't book right out of a brochure. Do your homework and ask questions."

Freidin, whose first VBT tour was a weekend inn-to-inn trip that cost just $43 (including meals), actually bemoans the popularization of luxury cycling trips. "People today want much more luxury," he explains. "They want private baths, no more than two people in a room, as many antiques and Laura Ashley fabrics as possible, and designer vegetables and fancy foods. These preferences have put the more human values of being a supportive group in a secondary position. I miss those days."

Freidin looks beyond the near future to a time when "luxury" will again describe the experience rather than the amenities.

"In some cases the second generation of tour company owners is more interested in profit than in the nature of what they're doing," he says. "They're maximizing the opportunity to make money rather than maximizing the nature of the experience. I didn't have to borrow any money when I started VBT. I had the luxury of concentrating on the quality of the experience I was providing to people. I suppose it will all come around again as values continue to change. People will realize it's always a luxury just to be treated well."

4 BED-AND-BREAKFAST (AND BIKE)

Got someone you want to introduce to touring? Here's a unique (and totally pampered) way to experience California, Oregon . . . or anywhere. It's written by Bicycling *editor Joe Kita, who took his wife, Maria, on a memorable auto/bike tour that included nightly stops at quaint and historic inns. When commercial tours may not be affordable or convenient, this is a way to do it yourself.*

Here's the dilemma. My wife and I have two weeks of vacation and a desire to see as much of the West Coast as possible. We want to ride in the most scenic places, of course, but also to unwind, kick back, eat well and be pampered. However, since Maria is a novice cyclist, the riding must be of a nature that will make this tour enjoyable while encouraging future ones. Obviously, 14 consecutive centuries would leave her (and me) more dazed than the typical Greyhounder. So what's an active couple to do?

Well, you begin by swallowing your pride and, gulp, renting a car. I know this insults the "true experience" tourists who routinely do thousand-mile treks with their entire lives bungied to their bikes, and for that I apologize. But for the vast majority of us with demanding jobs, limited leisure time and burgeoning families, that type of tour just isn't feasible anymore. A car and a couple of bikes afford the "express experience."

Our plan was to start in Anaheim, follow Highway 1 north along the famous California coast, turn inland at the Oregon border toward Crater Lake and Mount Hood, and then—about 1,800 miles later—fly home from Portland. We'd explore each town we stayed in by bicycle and ride the most scenic parks, but whenever the terrain got mundane or we needed to make time, we'd stash the bikes in back.

With that established, the next step is balancing the sweat with the sumptuous. From experience, I knew that if I was going to ask my wife (or any novice) to ride daily, the inevitable soreness would have to be soothed by some posh lodging and fine dining. (This makes the novice not only forget the day's rigors but also feel guilty enough to do it again come morning.)

For our tastes, there are few more sumptuous lodgings than bed-and-breakfasts and country inns. As does a bicycle, these quaint establishments allow you to absorb the unique ambience of a community. What's more, they offer all the amenities of a hotel but without that hotel feel or (usually) price. Spending the night in one can be like visiting mother—knick-knacks in the hutch, family portraits on the walls, thick comforters on the bed and hearty "are you sure you've had enough?" breakfasts.

To pinpoint some of the best, we relied on the recommendations of friends, *Country Inns* magazine and three books: *Frommer's Bed & Breakfast North America, The Bed & Breakfast Guide,* and *Country Inns and Back Roads.* These are just a few of many similar titles in libraries and book-stores that would be just as useful. Most are arranged by state, with detailed information and/or reviews of hundreds of accommodations.

We picked the most intriguing ones—including a light-house near San Francisco and a newly built Victorian-style mansion in Eureka—and planned our route around them. We put no more than about 200 miles between nightly stops, which meant at most we had an afternoon of driving. This left plenty of time for morning and evening rides, in addition to spur-of-the-moment excursions.

Although a travel agent can save time and aggravation when planning, using one is yet another way people dis-tance themselves from their destinations. It's fun and edu-cational to study road maps and page through travel guides and talk to chambers of commerce. And that's how we went about it.

To handle the diverse riding conditions we'd encoun-ter, we chose a pair of Giant 890i "all-terrain/fitness/sport" bikes. Actually, they are a lot less complicated than they sound and were among *Bicycling*'s "Hottest Bikes" in 1990. Built of bonded carbon fiber and equipped with 21-speed Shimano drivetrains with easy-to-use Rapid Fire shifters, the bikes were elegantly functional. These $800 all-purpose machines enabled us to negotiate singletrack in the Pygmy Forest, climb steep rocky trails at Point Reyes National Sea-shore and whiz along the new bike path in Ojai. Of course, being hybrids, they had limitations at either end of the road and off-road performance spectrums. But for general use, they were ideal.

Early October is a perfect time to see this part of the country. Most of the motorhomes are gone from Highway 1 and some inns are almost vacant. Yet the weather is often summerlike and the coastal fog but a wisp.

So here are the highlights of our trip, starting with the California destinations. Duplicate all or part of it next fall, or plan a similar tour in another part of the country. Such a vacation is tempting and flexible enough to lure even the softest couch potato. And who knows? Along the way, he or she just might realize how enjoyable bike touring can be.

Davis Home, Whittier. Every trip to southern California should begin with a visit to Disneyland. It is so clean, so happy, so upbeat and so much fun that when you leave you're Disneyfied in a way similar to the help. Even rush hour on "the 5" won't irritate you. On a typical autumn weekday, lines are short and you'll be able to do all the main attractions. You'll also get quite a workout—aerobic from walking, anaerobic from dodging kids in mouse ears waving frozen bananas.

For the first night of our trip, we stayed at the Davis Home in nearby Whittier. This bed-and-breakfast is located in a fairly exclusive hillside community called Rideout Heights, about five minutes from Whittier College. It has four tastefully decorated but smallish rooms with a private rear patio and a front deck that offers beautiful sunsets, nightlights and (on a clear day) ocean views. For $55 to $75 (including an ample breakfast), it's an economical alternative to the L.A. hotels. Nearby is Sycamore Canyon, a wildlife preserve where you can hike or bike.

Casa de La Luna, Ojai. Bud Scott, wearing a T-shirt, suspenders and bandanna, looked askance at our bikes. "If I ever get the urge to jog or do anything like that, I just sit down 'til it passes," he said.

Bud, who is in his seventies, stays fit through hard work and natural living, as does his wife, Doris. The Scott family built most of Casa de La Luna, a bed-and-breakfast ranch in Ojai, also known as "House of the Moon." The main building, where the family lives, has huge guestrooms and an aviary adjacent to the dining area. In fact, canaries provide the breakfast music. The ranch itself comprises seven acres of macadamia nut and orange orchards. There's even an art gallery, a china-painting workshop, and a number of private cottages, including one that Bud is outfitting as a honeymoon suite "with all that exotic stuff." According to Bud, Barbra Streisand and William Hurt have stayed at his place. All for a reasonable $65 to $95 a night.

Not far from the ranch is a paved bicycle trail that runs eight miles from downtown Ojai to Foster Park. Plans are to extend it south to Ventura and east to Santa Paula. Since it's a gradual descent out of Ojai, Bud says the best time to ride is late afternoon. This way, he winks, you're assured a tailwind on the way back.

Pickford House, Cambria. When you're riding on rural roads in the East, you must be watchful of dogs, squirrels and the occasional groundhog. But just outside of Cambria, our path was blocked by a tarantula. Since it was too small to bash with a pump and didn't respond to my firm commands of "Go home!" I did the manly thing and let my wife go first. (After all, I was on assignment.) Luckily, the tarantula lost interest and sauntered away.

Actually, this was the most traffic we encountered on a beautiful out-and-back ride that began at the Pickford House, a unique bed-and-breakfast with a silent screen–era motif. There's the Mary Pickford Room and others named after Douglas Fairbanks, Rudolph Valentino, Ethel Barrymore, Clara Bow, Norma Talmadge, Lillian Gish and Harold Lloyd. From here, we descended a steep hill into town, turned right onto Main Street and followed Santa Rosa Creek Road. This winds past cattle ranches and Linn's Farm (the birthplace of the olallieberry) to eventually become a thin, tree-canopied road that could pass for a bike path.

After 30 miles, we returned to find Cambria swallowed by a cold, coastal fog that gave a surreal feel to the eclectic community. We browsed through the downtown art shops and dined oceanside at a salty dog galley called the Sea Chest. If you sit at the oyster bar, the cook may toss you a wayward crab leg or scallop. Plus, you can read the walls to find such lore as "Billy ate 88 clams on 8-8-88."

Green Lantern Inn, Carmel. Curious as to how much money can actually be made in the publishing biz, we visited the 100,000-acre estate of newspaper mogul William Randolph Hearst in San Simeon, a short ride from Cambria. A bus, chattering with rollicking music from the 1920s and 1930s, carries you skyward (1,600 feet above the coastal plain) to his monument to excess. The mansion contains swimming pools built to create optical illusions, dinner tables as long as bowling alleys, a museum's worth of paintings, books and tapestries, and even a private theater. In fact, the castle is so big that there are four two-hour tours to different parts of it.

From San Simeon to Carmel, Highway 1 is a twisting serpent of road that winds high above the Pacific. While we saw many cyclists, the route can be as perilous as it is pretty. Narrow to nonexistent shoulders combined with fog, blind corners and (seemingly blind) motorhome jockeys make for stressful riding.

It's far better to speed ahead to Carmel and cycle the famous 17-Mile Drive on the Monterey Peninsula. This route winds past the crashing Pacific and some of the most famous golf courses in the world, including Pebble Beach and Spyglass. Plus, there are magnificent cypress groves and spectacular homes with storybook names such as "Paradise Found" and "Once Upon a Time. . . . " However, the roads are privately owned and there are strict regulations as to their use. Bikes are only permitted through certain gates, and you'll have to pay an entry fee and sign a release.

Afterward, save plenty of time for shopping and sightseeing in downtown Carmel, where the beautiful people browse. Our lodging this night was a smallish cottage at the Green Lantern Inn. But then again, after seeing the Hearst Castle and Monterey estates, your perspective gets a bit distorted.

East Brother Light Station, Point Richmond. Some people eat to ride, but I'll admit that I ride to eat. So being one of the culinary capitals of the world, it's fortunate that San Francisco is adjacent to some of the best off-road riding in the country, notably the Marin Headlands and Mount Tamalpais. In fact, it was here that mountain biking was born. But because of ongoing problems, there are strict regulations as to where bikes are permitted and even how fast they can go, so abide by the signs and be respectful of other trail users. For an equally exhilarating ride on pavement, try Pan Toll Road, the scenic stretch of blacktop where many car commercials are filmed.

Then after you're pleasantly thrashed, head for East Brother Light Station in San Pablo Bay. Make reservations well in advance because this is one of the finest, most unique bed-and-breakfasts anywhere. Built in 1874, it's actually a nonprofit historical site, which a group of local preservationists saved from demolition. Working nights and weekends, they eventually restored the gingerbread structure and opened a four-bedroom inn in 1980.

The first thing you'll notice after being shuttled across the bay is that this is a working light station, which means every 30 seconds (24 hours a day) a loud monotone sounds. On second thought, loud isn't actually the truest description. How about an entire Metallica album condensed into one 3-second blast?

The strange thing is that with the help of a five-course gourmet dinner, four different types of wine and friendly conversation around a communal table, that abrasive horn becomes a soft, reassuring lullaby by night's end.

East Brother is pricey (about $150 per person), but this includes two meals and a few choice ghost stories, all expertly prepared and delivered by Leigh Hurley, the station's keeper. Although the logbook told of 70-mile-per-hour winds and heavy seas, our night there was as placid as a Caribbean evening.

Timberhill Ranch, Jenner. Two of the cycling highlights of the trip were Point Reyes National Seashore and Salt Point State Park. The former is just north of San Francisco on Highway 1 and it, too, was one of the original playgrounds of the mountain bike. But restrictions have been tightened here as well, to the point where only certain out-and-back routes remain open to cyclists.

We stopped at the visitors' center in Olema for a map and then explored the Bear Valley and Fivebrooks trails. The latter is tunneled by ferns and giant redwoods, but it's a long, steep climb to the Pacific. Maria couldn't make it, we got into an argument, and the result is we now own a $3,000 tandem. So be careful.

After an ill-fated stop at the Tomales Bay Oyster Farm (only $4 a dozen, but did you ever try opening one?), we drove 13 miles into the hills toward Jenner and the Timberhill Ranch. This is more than a bed-and-breakfast. It's a country resort with private cabins, pool, tennis courts, Jacuzzi, stables and even personalized matchbooks to light your fire. It's pricey (about $135 per person), but that includes three gourmet meals. Our five-course dinner started, for instance, with caviar, proceeded through entrées of lamb and pheasant, ended with chocolate mousse and was doused by two bottles of chardonnay.

But again, there's some great riding nearby to balance the opulence. Back when the Coors Classic expanded into California, it sped by on these very roads during the Santa

Rosa-to-Guerneville stage. For off-road enthusiasts there's the nearby Kruse Rhododendron Reserve. In the spring, the rocky four-mile descent through it to the sea is perfumed by pink and purple blossoms. Salt Point State Park is even more fun. We didn't see one person in two hours of riding, which included some singletrack through the Pygmy Forest, a miniature woods.

MacCallum House, Mendocino. Although it's tough to leave Timberhill, you must get to Mendocino before five o'clock so you can visit its 99 boutiques and art galleries. We spotted about $11,000 worth of stuff we'd like to own, but even with an expense account you can only spend so much.

Mendocino is the type of town where you get a table by the window and just watch. And that's how we spent the evening at the MacCallum House, a beautifully warm bed-and-breakfast/restaurant/bar built in 1882. Sipping coffee and savoring raspberry eclairs with espresso ice cream, we watched a homeless man check into a dumpster for the night, a dozen or so BMWs parallel park, an assortment of deadheads truck down the road and a stunning blonde in an evening gown tweak the carburetor on her VW Beetle. If the season is right, you can even do some whale watching, as their annual spring migration follows this coast. In fact, the whale sculpture in front of MacCallum House is its trademark.

In all, we spent four hours in the Grey Whale Bar. Our trip was already half over, and it was proceeding nicely. Despite an occasional skirmish, my wife and I were enjoying cycling together. And if her legs got too tired or I got too frustrated waiting for her, there was always that inviting inn down the road to balance the biking. On this night, for instance, we bundled ourselves against the sea mist, hustled back to our cottage and lit a fire in our tiny potbelly stove.

Carter House, Eureka. Two miles north of Mendocino is Russian Gulch State Park. It lacks the large-scale grandeur of Point Reyes, but it's just as beautiful. A wide, well-kept trail winds 2½ miles into the gulch. It's a short, comfortable cruise, after which you can park your bikes and hike a few miles more to a waterfall.

Don't spend all your time here, though. Seaside paths at the other end of the park lead to several amazing geological formations. A punch bowl, for instance, is a giant hole in the ground into which the ocean ebbs and flows through sea caves. Even more spectacular are blowholes. In harsh weather, the ocean roars through a cave and explodes upward through holes in the rock. We spent about two hours here captivated by the scenery, as deer watched us from afar and painters watercolored the morning.

Since we wanted to reach Eureka in time to do some cycling there, we kept the bikes in the car as we hurtled northward with the logging trucks on Highway 101. There are numerous state parks along the way, however, that would afford spectacular riding, such as the Humboldt Redwoods and Avenue of the Giants.

Eureka was fogged in at 3:00 P.M., making the Carter House, a newly built Victorian-style mansion, appear eerily inviting. We took the recommendation of the co-owner and cycled through the suburbs to Sequoia Park. To our eastern eyes, this was one remarkable city park. Located in a residential area across from a school, it comprises a zoo with kangaroo and elk and a grove of giant sequoia trees. There's a paved loop in the park and also some footpaths through the woods and rhododendron groves.

We also explored the harbor and downtown by bike. In fact, our two wheels let us quickly experience a good part of the city. The waterfront is undergoing a rebirth of sorts, with new shops and carriage rides. Plus, there are some good seafood restaurants such as Gilhooeys, where the snapper and prawns come right off the boat and the fat oysters are locally grown.

The Carter House is a special place to settle into at the end of a day. There's always a fire blazing in the sitting room and classical music wafting through the halls. Since you meet the other guests at an evening wine and cheese gathering, friendly chatter is natural. And for breakfast the next morning there's a gourmet four-course meal garnished with exotic herbs and edible flowers.

Jacksonville Inn, Jacksonville, Oregon. This Oregon settlement is a former gold-mining town where the saloons still have swinging doors and the tombstones in the cemetery read, "He was a brave pioneer." In fact, our stay co-incided with the arrival of a movie crew that was preparing to dump dirt on California Street and board the shop windows.

We took a two-hour ride on Old Stage Road toward Gold Hill. This was the route of the Wells Fargo Stage Coach, and it's designated for bicycling, although the shoulder is narrow and the locals heavy-footed. The view is tremendous, though, as snow-capped peaks loom in the distance.

Our bed-and-breakfast this night was the landmark Jacksonville Inn, which remains the town hub. Built in 1863, it houses a gourmet restaurant, an extensive wine shop and cozy rooms with Western antiques and canopied beds. The original sandstone walls in the dining area even have specks of gold in the mortar.

For all its rough-and-tumble appearance, Jacksonville has a sophisticated side, too. There is a nationally famous Shakespeare festival in nearby Ashland, and the town itself has a large theater. There's also a hominess to it all that invites passing smiles and idle conversation with strangers. For instance, at breakfast the next morning we met a gentleman who raised Great Danes. He was on his way to San Francisco with a puppy, and we talked of local sites and other inns. That's the thing about bed-and-breakfasts—you make friends. When anybody says something to me in the lobby of a chain motel, I get suspicious.

Mirror Pond House, Bend, Oregon. Occasionally during an Oregon October you get a sapphire of a day. We enjoyed this one 8,000 feet above sea level at Crater Lake National Park. The sun was warm, the wind was light and most of the tourists were gone, leaving us to cycle the 33 rolling miles around its rim in near solitude. And I have never experienced anything more awesome.

The lake was formed when a volcano collapsed into itself and gradually filled with water. It's the darkest of blues and is said to be almost 2,000 feet deep, with warm springs and mysterious marine life lurking in its depths. The surrounding landscape is dotted with other volcanoes, high desert and, far below, rolling woodland. In all, it's one of those natural cathedrals where you tend to speak in whispers. On a bike, it can be almost dizzying.

From here, we drove to Bend and a homey little bed-and-breakfast called Mirror Pond. From its backyard you can feed swans and ducks, fish for trout and watch autumn slowly color the park's aspens. You're just a few minutes from downtown and about two miles from some more good riding. Ask Beryl, the owner, to point you toward Shevlon Park. You'll be passed by some trucks on the highway that leads there, but it's a designated bike route, so most drivers are courteous. We turned left into the park and followed a paved trail that eventually turned to dirt and then single-track as the surrounding gulch narrowed. Again, early in the morning at this time of year we met nary a soul. And when we returned to Mirror Pond, there was an ample breakfast awaiting us.

State Street Inn, Mount Hood, Oregon. From Bend, it's a scenic three-hour ride through Indian reservations and national forest to Mount Hood. We had the windows rolled down and country-and-western music blaring from the radio. However, Mount Hood is not the least bit pink-necked. Perched above the Columbia River Gorge, it's the wind-surfing capital of the United States, and that rock-'n'-roll lifestyle pervades everything in town. Nearly every car has a roof rack bristling with sporting equipment, and you wonder why the street signs aren't neon. There's windsurfing in the gorge, skiing in the mountains and, most important, great mountain biking in the surrounding hills.

A few places in town rent mountain bikes, and the experts there (or at any sport shop, for that matter) can direct you to the best trails. We parked about five miles out of town along the old, gravel/dirt Dalles Highway. From here, a network of rocky trails branches into the surrounding hills. It's intoxicating being perched so high above the river valley, with Mount Hood and, farther in the distance, Washington's Mount Adams as a backdrop.

There are a number of nice bed-and-breakfasts in this burgeoning town. We stayed at the State Street Inn, a recently renovated four-room guest house, where eggs Benedict and scones are the Sunday wakeup.

Corbett House, Portland, Oregon. Filled with the wistfulness that punctuates all trips, we lay in the grass amidst an Indian summer Sunday in Portland's Willamette Park.

That morning, after a dawn ride, we had followed the Columbia River Gorge west, taking the scenic detours whenever possible.

Our welcome was the Corbett House, about ten minutes from downtown. Eclectically decorated with a view of Mount St. Helens, it was our final home before heading home. With some reading material gleaned from the dusty shelves of the famous Powell bookstore, we wiled away the evening.

In two weeks we had ridden 300 miles, not a lot by regular touring standards, but enough to excite my wife about cycling. In fact, to ride for pleasure rather than purpose is not only the key to introducing someone to the sport but also the best way to refresh your interest in it as well.

5 CYCLING THE SKI RESORTS

For more than a thousand years, skiers had no choice but to climb every mountain they wanted to descend. Then, about 60 years ago, someone thought to rig a loop on a car engine and string it along pole tops to the crest of a hill. Voilà! The ski lift was born.

Soon, lifts of all kinds—some of them miles long—were erected on tall peaks everywhere. Skiing boomed as thousands of people who didn't have the stamina or inclination to climb enjoyed the lift up and ride down. Purists grumbled, saying the true rewards of skiing downhill could only be appreciated by those who earned it.

Now a similar thing is happening with mountain biking. Ski areas, looking for a way to better utilize their facilities during warm-weather months, are adding bike-carrying hooks to their aerial gondolas and chair lifts. Their hope is that the success of downhill skiing will repeat itself as cy-

The resorts discussed in this chapter are for illustration only. Prices and policies that were in effect when it was written may have changed. Always check with a resort for current information.

clists who don't have the stamina or inclination to ride up will delight in going down. Again the purists are grumbling.

But the cyclists are coming. The numbers aren't yet that impressive—nothing like skiing's millions. But every weekend throughout the summer, thousands will visit ski resorts across the country. For fees ranging upward from $4 per day, they will be given bikes, maps, lift service, groomed trails and more. Others won't ride the lifts but will use the resorts as bases for off-road touring adventures.

Why Pay to Ride?

Ski resorts are in the business of making outdoor-minded people happy. Aside from skiing facilities, most offer convenient lodging, good restaurants and soothing amenities such as swimming pools and hot tubs—all in a spectacular natural environment.

When the snow melts, the great facilities and superb settings remain. As the grass and wildflowers rise, prices fall. To attract visitors, resorts get resourceful by creating special events. Telluride, Colorado, for example, hosts nearly a dozen summer festivals celebrating such diverse interests as bluegrass music, wine, mushrooms, films, hang gliding and mountain biking.

For culture and comfort, it's easy to appreciate what ski areas offer. But for actual mountain biking, it's not so obvious. The question is, why pay to ride when there are ample opportunities to pedal off-road for free?

Well, not all cyclists want to camp or drive to a trail-head each morning. And for some, cycling is just *one part* of a vacation that includes time spent relaxing, swimming, hiking and eating well. The idea of arriving at a resort, parking the car and not seeing it again until you leave is appealing.

Alpine mountain biking is a robust sport that demands fairly high fitness and coordination. For those who have it, the rewards are tremendous. For those who don't, the options used to be level fire roads or the rare, nonintimidating, flat singletrack. But now, with ski resorts, there are new options and the possibility that thousands of unlikely candidates will be introduced to the pleasures of off-road riding.

Here's a look at three of the most progressive ski resorts in the country for mountain biking. What they're doing will give you an idea of the possibilities. Check with others in your region, and you'll likely be surprised at the opportunity they provide for day-long and weekend mountain bike tours.

Mammoth Mountain Bike Park: made to order. Let's make one thing clear: Alpine ski trails aren't much fun on mountain bikes. They're usually too steep, often too rocky and occasionally too wet. That's why resorts such as Mammoth Mountain in Mammoth Lakes, California, are creating trails on their property specifically for mountain bikes.

Mammoth started to recognize the potential in the mid 1980s when it began offering bike rentals and guided off-road cycling tours three times daily. "We couldn't keep up with the demand," says Jennifer Renner of Mammoth Adventure Connection, the resort's summer marketing agency. "Then we created mountain bike vacations."

A network of maintenance roads already existed, as did the Kamikaze Trail, the famous downhill used for national and international competition. The resort purchased a tractor to build trails. The result is a broad, challenging and ever-growing network.

Mammoth Mountain Bike Park opened in 1990. It includes nearly 60 miles of trails within the ski area's 3,500 acres, and it's 80 percent singletrack. Plus, at the base of the mountain is a dual slalom course with timing facilities. There's also a BMX course designed mainly for kids, and an obstacle arena with a variety of ride-over challenges.

For a $15 daily fee, cyclists can use all of these facilities and have unlimited use of Mammoth's two-stage gondola to the 11,053-foot summit, where several other trails begin. For $10, they can ride everything except the lift. Mammoth maintains a fleet of 60 rental bikes.

Vail's Grand Traverse: biking thrills at 10,000 feet. Thanks to its prime location (two hours west of Denver), great snow (400 inches annually) and massive investment in lifts, lodging and other facilities, Vail, Colorado, has become the most popular U.S. ski area.

In recent years Vail began to apply its resources and marketing savvy to off-road cycling. Three of its high-speed lifts have special carriers for mountain bikes, with a fee of $10 per day. Mountain bikes are available for rent in Vail Village and at Eagle's Nest (elevation: 10,250 feet).

Vail's marked mountain bike trail system includes the Little Eagle practice area for beginners, a pair of 5½-mile forested descents from the summit, several intermediate loops and a couple of expert grinds. One is Kloser's Klimb, a 2.4-mile loop with 1,000 feet of elevation gain. Experts ride it to compare their time with that of world mountain bike championship medalist Mike Kloser, a Vail resident. In all, there are about 20 miles of signed trails, with another 9 at Beaver Creek, Vail's sister resort.

One unusual Vail offering is its obstacle course at Eagle's Nest. It's set up like a golf course, with nine trials courses. Each is rated for difficulty. For instance, on the par twos, a pair of foot touches are standard and anything less is superb.

Vail's most ambitious project is the Grand Traverse, a 14-mile trail that will circle the ski area at about 10,000 feet. While the entire loop is still being finished, the first 4-mile section was opened in 1991. Graded with a small bulldozer, the Grand Traverse is wider than singletrack but narrower than a service road.

Mount Snow's Off-Road School: for trail-riding techniques. Mount Snow Resort in southern Vermont opened its Mountain Bike School and Touring Center in 1988. The concept grew from the fact that trail riding required techniques and a backcountry awareness that most people, even road cyclists, don't have. So Mount Snow purchased a fleet of mountain bikes for use as rentals, mapped 140 miles of unpaved roads and trails within a 10-mile radius of the base of the mountain, arranged for complete instruction/lodging packages and opened for business.

During the first four years, the focus of Mount Snow's cycling program has evolved. For example, the resort has hosted Saturday afternoon time trials on the same course used for the National Off-Road Bicycling Association (NORBA) National Championship Series finals. And guided tours—from two hours to several days—have become popular.

Mount Snow doesn't operate its lifts for cyclists or charge a fee for using its trails, however. Revenue comes from school tuition, guide fees, rentals and its bike shop. A two-day session at the school costs $119 ($136 if you also rent a bike).

Other Opportunities Closer to Home

For city dwellers who search in vain for good, uncrowded, legal trail riding near home, "urban" resorts offer much promise. Even small ski areas located near big cities have about 50 acres of land, which is plenty for marking a varied trail network.

Two hours from Los Angeles, for instance, Snow Summit ski area operates its Sky Chair through the summer. It rises 1,200 feet to the View House restaurant that oversees Big Bear Lake—the starting point for 60 miles of trails, plus more on adjoining forest service land.

But while alpine resorts are embracing the mountain bike option in the off-season, cross-country ski areas are lagging behind. Although their terrain and trails are better suited to riding, they lack the resources.

"It's difficult to just charge for using the trails," says Jonathan Weisel of Nordic Group International, a research and consulting group for cross-country ski areas. "Dozens of resorts are looking into it, but everyone is skeptical. You really need a guide service, lifts and a fleet of rentals, which cost money. And you have to pay the people who maintain the area and the bikes."

Nevertheless, check with the cross-country ski areas in your locale. As mountain biking has grown in popularity, more Nordic resorts have begun catering to cyclists. The riding can be terrific, and the accommodations more rustic and natural than at big downhill ski centers.

For further information on the resorts discussed in this chapter, contact Mammoth Mountain Bike Park, Box 353, Mammoth Lakes, CA 93546; Mount Snow, The Mountain Bike School, 600 Mountain Rd., Mount Snow, VT 05356; Vail Associates, Inc., Box 7, Vail, CO 81658.

Part Two

THE U.S. TRANS-CONTINENTAL

6 A RIDE OF PASSAGE

The transcontinental. For many cyclists, it's the ultimate dream—pedaling from coast to coast and experiencing all that America offers. For some, the challenge is in crossing at a rapid pace with a group of like-minded riders, as is done each summer on the 21-day Pacific-Atlantic Cycling (PAC) Tour (for information write to Box 73C, Harvard, IL 60033). For many others, the experience comes with a larger, more leisurely group, perhaps as a fund-raising ride for charity. And then there are those who go it alone or with a friend, as David M. Abramson did several years ago. In the following account, he explains why he found cross-country touring much more poetic than heroic.

What does it feel like to ride a bicycle across the country? Nobody ever asked me that. Eighteen states, 4,500 transcontinental miles, and all anyone wanted to know was:

- "How many tires you gone through on that thing?" This, with a knowing nod at the rolling luggage rack I called a bicycle, straining under 50 pounds of loaded panniers.
- "Where the hell do you sleep?" They didn't always want to stick around for the complete answer. "Well, sir, we've slept under the stairway of a fast-

food chicken place with Jimmy Joe and Mary Sue flirting overhead, under the wings of a Piper Cub in a hangar/barn, on a waterbed in some bachelor pad in Muscatine, Iowa, on village greens, beaches, half-constructed condos. . . . Wait! Don't go away, we're not finished!"

- "Why in the world are you pedaling a bicycle (i.e., toy) across America?" Did they really want to hear my life story? Did they really want to know I'd dreamed of this trip since age 11, when I first rode my Schwinn 3-speed beyond the neighborhood and had my initial vision of unlimited travel? Did they want to hear my blather of the great metaphor of linking two bodies of water? Or did they want me to explain why I was so unhinged, so contrary to the mainstream tourist—why I couldn't just fly like everybody else.

And then my interlocutors would invariably say: "I could never do anything like that. I can barely bicycle around the block."

Of course, they were wrong. Anyone can cycle across the country. You can do it in a matter of weeks if you like, or make it a multimonth journey, as I did. Either way, as you become a creature of the road it mostly feels mundane. It takes perspective to erase the routine and recall all the glory moments, all the wondrous feelings of uninhibited travel and of distance that become a physical part of you, like an extra network of tendons and blood vessels in your legs. It doesn't feel heroic to cross the continent; it feels poetic.

Remembering the Coast-to-Coast Experience

That's from the distance of seven years. When *Bicycling* asked me to share my thoughts on cross-country cycling, I dug out my journals and map—with its faded pink highway and my highlighted route snaking from New York City through New Jersey and Pennsylvania, the Allegheny Mountains, the Great Plains, the rising plateau of dust-dry Colorado, the Rocky Mountains and the Continental Divide, the rush to the Pacific in Oregon and the final roller-coaster ride to the western edge of the continent in San Francisco—and I remembered what it felt like.

Like the first day, for instance. Christopher, my traveling partner, and I left Manhattan on a hot July morning. We were leaving behind our apartments and, to some extent, past lives. We had only vague notions of ever returning. However sophisticated we were to the pulse of New York City, we were utterly ignorant of the heartland's beat, and we wanted to experience the country firsthand. Like Albert Brooks in *Lost in America,* we wanted to go out and "touch an Indian."

We had maps, but we had no plan. Midspan on the George Washington Bridge we stopped to look back at Manhattan. We knew the next major suspension bridge we crossed would be the Golden Gate. Until then, we planned to wing it, to live at the mercy of our whims and the hospitality of strangers. The Hudson River rippled below us, the expansion plates of the bridge clanging under the heavy rush-hour load, the whole walkway seeming to sway slightly in the wind. This was day one of an unknown number of days, weeks and months, through unknown territory, with a caveat of "forward, no return." I'll tell you how it felt. Terrifying.

The first fortnight was our bicycle boot camp, our initiation into life on the road. We needed to acclimate to the equipment, conform to the saddles, ready our bodies for an average of 70 miles a day and overcome all the childhood exhortations not to talk to strangers. As we gradually immersed ourselves in the country, it revealed itself in the kindness of people who invited us into their homes (often unsolicited) and the curiosity of others met along the way. One memorable stranger was the pot-bellied fellow in rural Maryland with the Confederate tie pin who interrupted our lunch in a supermarket parking lot.

"Where you boys from?"

"New York, en route to San Francisco."

"Ay-yup, I did that once myself. Back in the 1930s before they had any of these newfangled bikes. I went from

Virginia to San Diego. Had to damn near walk up those Rockies with my 1-speed. Whenever I ran out of money I'd go to a restaurant and ask for a job. Never got turned down, either. I'd get $3, a place to sleep, and all I could eat."

For a brief moment, Chris and I felt like newly sworn members of some great universal cross-country club. We may have been half a century removed from this pioneer, yet we shared his spirit of adventure. And he sure knew what it felt like.

An All-Encompassing Adventure

For us, cycling the country was more than a vacation, or a means of getting from one coast to the other or a mere physical challenge. For that, there were plenty of harder things we could have done, like biking all the 14,000-foot Rocky Mountain peaks. Instead, a cross-country trip appealed to our sense of the gestalt. It allowed us to see the country on our own motive power and feel the weight of each region passing through us.

To talk of the westerly winds that blow unimpeded across the plains states is one thing; to bicycle headlong into them offers a new realm of understanding. Especially when you know that soon it will be time to climb the mountains, breathe thinner air (we nodded out on a roadside table at 8,500 feet), play tag with afternoon thunderstorms and dance about a fire at night to keep warm.

America has a long heritage of cross-country travel. Chris and I imagined ourselves fitting into a world that included not only cyclists but trappers and fur-traders, Lewis and Clark, wagon-borne pioneers, Dust Bowl emigrants, railroad tramps, young men going west, long-distance truckers, Dharma Bums, Merry Pranksters, even the retired "snowbirds" in Airstreams. Still, the road is often lonely.

In Benkelman, Nebraska, for instance, Chris and I were feeling adrift—so far from home and so far from our destination. This was compounded by the fact that many midwesterners regarded us as aliens. Pulling into small towns, wearing Lycra shorts and cleated shoes, we were gawked at and rarely approached. Except for Cecil. He was a crop duster in his forties, a man who had traded a steady airline job, a wife and a family for the daredeviltry of low-altitude flying. By his own accounts he was an outsider, adrift in his own world. He invited us into his home and told us of the canary-yellow Turbin Thrush he flew, sometimes so low the tires brushed the fields.

The next morning at dawn, Cecil woke us so we could cycle to the hangar and see his plane. With sleepy eyes we marveled at its blunt-nose sleekness, thanked him again for his graciousness and departed.

Forty miles and four hours later, Chris and I were riding along a secondary road in Kansas when we heard an approaching rumble. Instinctively, we moved onto the shoulder to let the tractor-trailer pass. None did. The rumble grew louder. Then with a heart-stopping whoosh, a canary-yellow crop duster passed 20 feet above our heads, tipped its wings in salute and banked east over the corn and soybean fields. It was Cecil, saying goodbye.

Partners by Chance in a Shared Dream

Chris and I hadn't known each other before our trip. I had picked his name from the bulletin board at a local youth hostel. Fortunately, we shared many things. We were both in our early twenties. He was a photographer and artist, I was a writer. We were both reeling from long-term romances gone bad and we were both chasing new lives. By the time we reached the Pacific Ocean we had both decided to relocate in California. By then, after nearly three months on our bikes, we felt as if we carried all our belongings with us anyway, like carpetbaggers on two wheels.

We also felt like an old married couple. We had stared at each other for 87 breakfasts and shared a leaky tent for 87 nights. There came a point in Wyoming where we squabbled and talked of splitting and finishing the trip alone. But our dream of the Golden Gate had been a shared vision from the first day on the George Washington Bridge. We made amends and agreed to continue.

Our final day was long (95 miles), and we didn't reach Sausalito until near dusk. I can still recall how it felt when we rounded the bend and saw the Golden Gate Bridge for the first time. The sun was setting and the Marin headlands, craggy palisades that front the Pacific, had deepened to the same reddish-orange hue as the span. We had waited three months for this moment, anticipated it, prayed for it on the hottest, windiest days, and now it was upon us. We didn't want the trip to end, yet we didn't want to go any farther.

This Calls for a Toast!

We crossed the bridge slowly with the sun setting to our right. Neither of us said a word. When we reached the end of the bridge it was dark, but the lights of San Francisco illuminated the sky.

Our crossing was done, but we felt it wasn't yet complete. Somehow, the weight of the trip was still upon us, as if we were Odysseus sailing into his home port. It needed some sort of ritual to symbolize its end. Since it was too dark to ride we hailed a cab, loaded our bikes in and directed the driver to a downtown bar where a friend of a friend awaited us. When we arrived we unloaded our equipment. A young guy with blond hair down to his waist approached us.

"Where are you coming from?"

We told him. But our New York guard had returned and we were suspicious of his friendliness.

"Hey, I'm from New York, too. Welcome to San Francisco." He threw his arms around us and gave both of us a hug. A guy with checkered pants and a brown paper bag walked by. The blond turned and said: "These guys just biked across country!"

The guy in the checkered pants looked at us, looked at our bikes and smiled. He said: "This calls for a toast." He reached into the bag, unscrewed the cap and passed the firewater around. When we'd all taken a swig he wished us luck and went on his way. I'm not sure that's what Odysseus had waiting for him, but as far as Chris and I were concerned, our journey was complete. It felt, finally, like we were home.

7 PLANNING YOUR JOURNEY

There are five things you must take with you when you ride across America. Bikecentennial, a national organization designed to promote touring, discovered these things the hard way—by putting thousands of cyclists on transcontinental tours for more than a dozen years. Of all the essentials for saving time and frustration in cross-country planning, these five are most important. Don't leave home without:

1. A good route.
2. Adequate time and money.
3. Physical preparedness.
4. Proper equipment.
5. The right attitude.

First and Foremost: A Good Route

The two most popular cross-country routes are the TransAmerica Bicycle Trail (4,250 miles) and the Northern Tier Bicycle Route (4,400 miles), both developed by Bikecentennial. Following such predesigned routes assures you of good cycling roads and of having detailed maps that note point-to-point mileage and the availability of food, water and accommodations.

Mapping your own route may allow you to visit friends and particular places of interest, but such freedom has its price. In parts of the west, for instance, where roads are scarce, you may find yourself jockeying with 18-wheelers and speeding cars. Some states even prohibit bicycles on their interstates. It's nice to know beforehand.

If you decide to plan your own route, it's best to do most of your cycling on country and secondary roads. Although such a route will undoubtedly be less direct, you'll have a more pleasant and scenic trip. One good source of

Prices that were in effect when this chapter was written may have changed. Always check with campgrounds, hostels, etc. for current information.

route information is county maps, available from state tourism offices. Since they can take up a lot of space in your panniers, it's best to trim away the unnecessary parts of the map. To further conserve space and weight when you're on the road, throw away each map when you're done with it.

As for terrain, you're bound to face major climbs. Most transcontinental cyclists say the Rockies are easier to surmount than the Ozarks and the Appalachians. This is because the long but gradual western slopes encourage a rhythmic spin, while the more abrupt eastern mountains demand frequent gear changes and shifts in cadence.

As discussed in chapter 8, another major factor is the wind. It has a tendency to be especially fierce on the Plains, so make sure your bike is geared properly and your legs are well conditioned.

Where will you sleep? For accommodations, camping is the least expensive and most flexible option, but hostels and motels offer more comfort. Many cross-country cyclists combine the two—camping a few nights, then staying in a motel every third or fourth night.

Most bookstores carry the national campground directories published by Rand McNally and Woodall. The American Automobile Association (AAA) also sells one. Other sources of campground information include: state highway maps, the department of parks and recreation in each state, the U.S. Forest Service and the National Park Service. Also, don't overlook commercial facilities such as Kampgrounds of America (KOA). Although more expensive than public campgrounds, they have shower and laundry facilities. In addition, national and state parks often have camping facilities.

Hostels are a pleasant and inexpensive place to stay, plus a good way to meet fellow travelers. But don't plan on finding a hostel each night on a cross-country tour. Most are in New England, New York, Pennsylvania, Ohio, Michigan, Colorado and along the West Coast. For approximately $8 you're entitled to a bed, use of the kitchen and a shower. For more information about hostels worldwide, write American Youth Hostels, Box 37613, Washington, DC 20013-7613.

Motel directories are published by AAA and chains such as Motel 6 and Days Inn. Before you go, contact state tourism boards for their directories. If you're on the road and need reservations quickly, simply call the chamber of commerce or an operator in the next town and ask to be connected to a local motel. Bikecentennial's "Cyclists' Yellow Pages" is another good resource for accommodations. You can obtain ordering information for this and other helpful material by writing to Bikecentennial, Box 8308, Missoula, MT 59807.

Time and Money: How Much Have You Got?

Loaded touring, where you carry camping and cooking gear, usually costs about $15 per day ($5 for campsites, $10 for food). Light touring, where indoor accommodations are used, generally costs about $45 per day.

Most Bikecentennial groups cross the country in 90 days. They average 55 miles a day, with a rest day every week to week and a half. Therefore, a transcontinental camping tour generally costs $1,350 and a "light" tour just over $4,000. Using a variety of accommodations will put you somewhere in between.

Perhaps the best way to save money on a transcontinental trip is to travel with a friend. The prices just quoted are for one rider. Another cyclist will not only provide companionship and assistance but also reduce the cost of accommodations by 50 percent.

Whether you're traveling alone or with someone, budget an additional $8 a day for incidentals such as film, snacks, postage, souvenirs and beverages. Also, carry an emergency fund of at least $150, preferably in travelers checks, for unanticipated expenses.

Physical Preparedness

Inadequate training can ruin your grand adventure. To avoid struggling, especially early in the trip, begin gradual conditioning at least one month before departure. It isn't necessary to ride every day, but try to cycle at least four times a week. Assuming you're reasonably fit, go out for two to four hours each time and maintain a cadence of 75 to 90 rpms.

During your third and fourth weeks of preparation, do several day tours of 55 to 65 miles and at least one multiday dress rehearsal. Ride across varied terrain and do plenty of tough hills. Use the bike you'll be riding on tour, equipped with loaded packs. This way, you'll adapt to the bike and the load while making sure you're properly outfitted.

To start your trip, schedule a few short, easy days. This will give you additional time to make necessary adjustments and get into the rhythm of cross-country cycling.

Nutritionally, a transcontinental tour is a rare opportunity—a chance to eat as much as you want. Since you'll be burning approximately 3,000 to 5,000 calories a day, it's almost impossible to eat or drink too much. The best way to replenish your energy stores and ensure a constant supply of fuel is to eat before you're hungry and drink before you're thirsty. Of course, this isn't a license to pedal from one fast-food joint to the next. Instead, you should aim for a daily caloric intake comprised of 65 percent carbohydrate, 25 percent fat and 10 percent protein. Keep handy a supply of gorp (a homemade mixture of raisins, peanuts, M&Ms and such), granola, fig bars or other quick-energy food.

Proper Equipment: Gears, Etc.

Wheels and gearing are the most common sources of trouble on cross-country tours.

Leave your lightweight rims, tires and tubes at home. This is a tour, not the Race Across America. Most clincher tires narrower than 32C or 1¼ inches don't have enough strength or resiliency to withstand the abuse. You might be sacrificing the low rolling resistance of your racing rims and high-pressure tires, but you won't have to sit beside the campfire three nights a week replacing spokes.

To help select the wheels best suited for your combination of bike, load, riding technique and road surfaces, consult the professional wheelbuilder at your local bike shop. Most riders find the greatest reliability with high-quality, 14-gauge, stainless-steel spokes, such as those manufactured by Wheelsmith.

As for gearing, the key to extended touring is spinning the pedals rather than straining against them. To facilitate this, you'll need gears that allow you to maintain a cadence of 75 to 90 rpm whether you're climbing the Rockies, cruising on the Plains or battling a stiff Missouri headwind.

Most neophyte tourists err by overgearing. A bike that's suitable for bed-and-breakfast touring might not be geared properly to handle fully loaded panniers. An 18- or 21-speed system should provide enough alternatives for any situation. The low gears should be in the 20- to 30-inch range, with several evenly spaced midrange ratios of 35 to 70 inches. Above this, you'll only need a few "cranking gears" for those fortunate (and too few) days when you have a tailwind on the flats.

What to carry (and how to pack it). Regarding your load, carry no more than 40 to 50 pounds of equipment (much less if you're not camping). You'll need front and rear panniers and a handlebar bag. Some riders find their bike behaves best when about 40 percent of the weight is over the rear wheel and 60 percent is over the front; others find the opposite. Experiment to learn what works best for you. Reserve the handlebar bag for small, frequently used items such as a wallet, camera and munchies. Most handlebar bags are easily removed, so you can take your valuables along when you go into a cafe or grocery. Tools can be carried in a seat bag.

Bigger or heavier items should be stored in the front and rear panniers, except for your sleeping bag, pad and tent, which should be attached to the top of the rear rack with elastic cords. Clothing should be rolled, put in clear plastic bags (large, heavy-duty freezer bags work well) and packed vertically in one or two of the panniers. (Take extra bags for dirty clothes.) Your cooking gear can then go in the other panniers. With a little thought, you should be able to design an easy packing system that allows you to find what's needed without emptying your entire load. (See chapter 10 for a list of recommended items.)

For most people, the best bet in tents is a lightweight two-person model with screening for ventilation and a vestibule for storing equipment. Because you'll be spending some chilly mornings at high elevations, your sleeping bag should be rated for 32°F. A synthetic fill is economical and insulates well when damp, but a down fill is warmer, packs smaller and withstands repeated compressions better. A closed-cell foam pad is best for insulating you from the damp, cold earth. Even better, perhaps, is a thin, self-inflating pad (available at most sporting goods stores). It packs well and is more durable than regular air matresses, which inevitably leak and are poor insulators.

Most important, don't carry more gear than necessary. When packing, remember that you'll be lugging that hair dryer or backgammon set up each and every hill. So leave the frills at home.

The Right Attitude

Probably more cross-country tours are aborted because of a lack of mental preparedness than for any physical reason. The right attitude for such a journey includes a sense of humor and a thirst for adventure, plus adaptability. You must be prepared for anything, because on the backroads of America you're liable to find it. Rehearsal trips might help you get used to life on the road, but there's only one way to understand this remarkable mental and physical journey: Do it.

As you plan your dream tour, it will grow until it seems an overwhelming event. But once you're on the road, you'll stop thinking about the thousands of miles and focus instead on the 25 to go before lunch. The enormity of the trip is reduced by the routine. Of course, it just may be the best routine you'll ever experience.

8 FACTOR IN THE PREVAILING WINDS

America's fads move west to east. The Race Across America (RAAM) follows the same route. And when was the last time you heard of a storm system hurtling westward from New Jersey? Thus, when planning a cross-country bike tour, it makes sense to start on the Pacific coast and get those prevailing westerly currents behind you.

Or does it?

A closer look shows those westerlies aren't so prevailing after all. In fact, bucking the trend and pedaling east to west may be just as sensible.

Using statistics from the National Climatic Data Center (NCDC) in Asheville, North Carolina, meteorologists Tim and Jennifer Klingler studied the prevailing summer wind direction in more than 70 cities. From May through August, any time the wind came from between the southwest and northwest, it was noted as westerly. They then compared how often westerly and easterly winds prevailed. This led to their formulating a dominant summer wind direction for different areas of the country, which is illustrated in the map on page 50.

It's clear that in the country's heartland, wind more often comes from the east than west, while closer to the coasts it's more commonly west to east. Thus, the direction you decide to pedal depends largely on your desires. Do you want to have a tailwind at the beginning and end of your tour? If so, go west to east, But if you'd rather have some atmospheric assistance in the middle portion of your ride, go east to west. Of course, the map represents only averages, and on any given day you could encounter wind from any direction.

In the upper level of the atmosphere, westerly winds do predominate—which explains the weather patterns. But on the earth's surface, as the study shows, there's no such directional domination. However, the Klinglers' research in-

The light sections show areas where prevailing winds are commonly west to east. Darker sections show areas where east-to-west winds are more common.

volved only a west versus east wind comparison. When all four directions are considered, the data indicate that for much of the nation during the summer, the wind most frequently comes from the south. So actually, the best cross-country route is not from either sea but from the Gulf of Mexico to the Great Lakes.

9   CAMERAS AND DIARIES TO RECORD THE MEMORIES

Remember when you pedaled around that bend and saw the sunset you thought you'd never forget? Getting kind of dim, isn't it? With the right camera, however, or even a descriptive phrase in your diary, every memorable sight on a bike tour can be saved and savored for years. In this chapter, two veteran cyclists share their tips for preserving a cross-country trip on film and in words.

Byron Reed on Taking Pictures

It's been more than ten years since I rode across the United States on Bikecentennial's TransAmerica Trail. It was an experience I'll never forget, largely because of the many photographs I took. From the shot of Lazy Louie's bicycle camp near Hardville, Missouri, to the photo of my transcontinental partner and me at the trail's former official finish in Astoria, Oregon, each picture is a priceless vestige from an epic journey.

Capturing such moments on film can be tricky, however, especially given the unique rigors of a cross-country tour. You have to choose the right camera and film, learn how to take quality pictures and make sure your equipment isn't damaged. Despite the inconvenience, you'll no doubt find it all worthwhile when, years later, you page through your cross-country photo album.

Choosing the right camera. The equipment you select depends on the quality of images you desire. Simple snapshots taken under good conditions require relatively uncomplicated equipment. Many basic 35-mm cameras costing less than $100 will do the job.

The automatic focus 35-mm models are a bit nicer, though. These have automatic exposure control and built-in flash. Manufacturers such as Nikon, Olympus, Minolta, Canon and Pentax have models starting at around $120. Even as a professional photographer, I use an Olympus XA pocket camera when I don't want to carry large equipment.

New on the market is the throwaway camera. For less than $10 you get a cardboard camera that looks like a box of film with a lens on it. After taking 24 pictures, you simply give the entire package to a photo developer. Although you probably won't want this as your only camera for a cross-country tour, it's a nice complement to regular photo gear.

Since you'll only be sacrificing a few dollars if it's lost or damaged, you can use it in those risky places you wouldn't dare take a "real" camera.

For maximum flexibility and quality, the best choice is a 35-mm SLR (single-lens reflex) camera with several lenses. This type of camera has become smaller, lighter and more durable during the past few years. Although the camera itself usually costs about $250, each lens can be priced upwards of $300. Nevertheless, this system has several advantages.

First, since it has manual focusing, it's nearly impossible to get blurry shots. Sometimes, auto-focus cameras don't home in on the subject you want.

Second, you can substitute lenses to capture the photo you envision. I generally carry four lenses on a long tour: a 24-mm wide-angle, a 50-mm "normal" lens, a 135-mm short telephoto and a 200-mm telephoto. If I need to limit my equipment, I take only a camera body and a 35–105-mm zoom. This covers my favorite ranges.

While there are many camera brands to choose from, the name on your equipment isn't nearly as important as how you compose your photos and how well you understand your film.

Consider composition and film speed. Volumes have been written on photographic composition, but it can all be reduced to one question you should ask yourself before snapping every picture: "What's the subject of the photo I'm about to take?" Once you have the answer, eliminate extraneous matter. This takes self-discipline and practice. Don't be afraid to use film. The cost per frame is low compared to the time and effort it took to pedal to that perfect spot.

Regarding film, most cycling photos are taken during the day, so avoid the temptation to choose fast film (e.g., ASA 500), thinking you might shoot in low light. When used in normal light, high-speed film gives photos a grainy appearance. You'll get sharper, more colorful results with films in the ASA 64 to 100 range. If you do find yourself indoors or in low light, simply use a flash.

Protecting your investment. Whether you have an Instamatic or a top-of-the-line 35-mm model, long-distance touring puts unusual strains on camera equipment. For instance, on a cross-country trip, you'll have to weather a few storms. To avoid having your equipment damaged, seal all camera gear in plastic zip-shut bags. Had I learned this trick before six days of rain on my transcontinental trek, I would've saved the expense of repairing a fogged lens.

Vibration is another enemy of delicate camera mechanisms. The cumulative effect of bumping across more than 4,000 miles can be devastating. I remember fishing around in a pannier for my wide-angle lens and finding it in pieces because the tiny screw holding it together had vibrated loose. Needless to say, I missed the shot.

To dampen road shock, carry your equipment in a handlebar bag that has a support frame and elastic cords that fasten to dropout eyelets on the front fork. Since it's located between the curves of your handlebar, it'll be fairly well protected in case of a crash. Once I flipped end-over-end but my camera and lenses survived. Such an arrangement also keeps your equipment handy for those moments when the light is just right and the scenery spectacular. Another benefit is that a handlebar bag quickly converts to a shoulder bag—the perfect carrying case for off-bike travel.

To protect the pictures you've already taken, mail your film to a photo developer back home and arrange for future pick-up. Carrying rolls of exposed film adds weight. Plus, there's the risk of their being lost or damaged.

As you pedal across America, you'll see mountains, road signs, cities, general stores, farmers, truck stops, lakes, animals and other memorable sights. Although it might take a few minutes to stop and capture these moments, if you follow these tips the only photos you'll regret will be the ones you didn't take.

Alys Culhane on Keeping a Journal

I had just ridden across the country by myself. Being a woman on my first extended tour, I thought the experience would make a unique and exciting story. In fact, with my foolproof notekeeping, I was convinced it would be published by a national magazine and maybe even become a book.

But no one has ever read about my journey. The information I so painstakingly transcribed about miles ridden and towns visited wasn't enough. As a result, the notebook and my unfinished manuscript lie forgotten in some desk drawer.

Because of my mistakes, I learned how to keep a good journal. Actually, if you desire hours of reminiscent pleasure or usable facts for a book or article, there are only two things to remember: Be honest and be consistent.

Originally, I was self-conscious about writing my thoughts in a diary where anyone could read them. But in my later struggles to write about my cross-counry trip, I learned that personal observations are invaluable. They add life to factual information.

Take it slow and preserve details. And so, on my next tour—a ride through the Yukon to Fairbanks, Alaska—I deliberately went slow. Instead of being obsessed with "getting there," I lifted my nose from the handlebar and observed. For 15 minutes every two hours, I made myself get off the bike and write. This enabled me to see things I ordinarily would have missed and left me with more energy for cycling later in the day. Instead of just recording that I crossed the Top of the World Highway near Dawson City, I wrote about how tough it was. And rather than merely noting there were 14 miles of construction along the Taylor Highway, I explained the elation of riding through it on a mountain bike.

If 15 minutes of writing every two hours seems a bit much, devise a plan you find more convenient. For instance, if you're cycling in an area where the noon sun is insufferable, find a shady spot where you can lunch and write each day. Or, if you're too tired to write at day's end, reserve a few minutes each morning. Whatever time you choose, be consistent. Missing an entry one day makes it harder to write the next.

It's also useful and fun to keep a second journal—a scrapbook of tour memorabilia. Mine usually included clippings from local newspapers, postcards, hand-drawn maps, matchbook covers, anything that strikes my fancy—all pasted to the pages. At the end of a tour from Fairbanks to Portland, Oregon, my scrapbook contained, among other things, a recipe for sourdough pancakes, a crayon drawing of my bicycle from a child and a ferry ticket stub. I continued to add to it afterward, pasting in letters, postcards and photos. I've found it makes many parts of my route easier to remember.

If you have the talent, another good way to capture some memories is by drawing sketches. It's relaxing and enjoyable to sit by the road and sketch the countryside.

For those who don't like to write or draw, a small tape recorder carried in a jersey pocket will enable you to record your feelings quickly and effortlessly. You'll also capture some of natural background sounds of the tour. These will carry you back in time whenever you hear them.

10 WHAT TO PACK

We asked four long-distance cyclists to list items they take on a transcontinental tour. The kitchen sink didn't make this collection, but almost everything else did. Of course, you don't have to include every item when you fill your panniers. And unless you're camping, you won't need a lot of it. But, in any case, it's a good idea to ponder the preferences of a few old pros.

Here, then, is the cross-country cyclist's list of "essentials."

Clothing

☐ Bathing suit
☐ Cycling gloves
☐ Cycling jersey
☐ Cycling shoes
☐ Cycling shorts
   (2 pairs)
☐ Flip-flop sandals
☐ Hat
☐ Helmet
☐ Long-sleeve shirt
☐ Nylon foot warmers
☐ Pants

☐ Rain jacket
☐ Rain pants
☐ Short-sleeve shirts (2)
☐ Sneakers
☐ Socks (3 pairs)
☐ Sweater
☐ Sweatpants
☐ Tights
☐ T-shirts (4)
☐ Underwear (3 pairs)
☐ Windbreaker

Tools and Spare Parts

- ☐ 6-inch adjustable wrench
- ☐ Air gauge
- ☐ Allen wrenches
- ☐ Chain lubricant
- ☐ Chain rivet extractor
- ☐ 6-inch channel locks
- ☐ Crank puller
- ☐ Foldable spare tire
- ☐ Freewheel/cassette remover
- ☐ Grease cloth
- ☐ Pliers
- ☐ Screwdriver
- ☐ Spare ball bearings
- ☐ Spare brake pads
- ☐ Spare chain
- ☐ Spare rear brake cable
- ☐ Spare rear derailleur
- ☐ Spare rear derailleur cable
- ☐ Spare spokes
- ☐ Spare toe clip and strap
- ☐ Spare tubes (3)
- ☐ Spoke wrench
- ☐ Tire irons
- ☐ Tire patch kit
- ☐ Tire pump
- ☐ Tire valve adapter
- ☐ Wrenches (4-mm to 12-mm)

Cooking and Camping Paraphernalia

- ☐ Aluminum dish
- ☐ Aluminum frying pan
- ☐ Can opener
- ☐ Cooking oil
- ☐ Cooking pot
- ☐ Fork
- ☐ Freeze-dried meals (3)
- ☐ Matches
- ☐ Plastic spatula
- ☐ Pot scrubber
- ☐ Sleeping bag
- ☐ Sleeping pad
- ☐ Spoon
- ☐ Steel cup
- ☐ Stove
- ☐ Swiss army knife
- ☐ Tent

Recreational Equipment

- ☐ Binoculars
- ☐ Camera
- ☐ Camera lenses
- ☐ Film
- ☐ Film canisters
- ☐ Film mailers
- ☐ Frisbee
- ☐ Kite
- ☐ Playing cards
- ☐ Radio

Hygiene and First Aid

☐ Adhesive bandages
☐ Antibacterial first-aid
   cream
☐ Aspirin
☐ Chamois lubricant
☐ Cotton swabs
☐ Dental floss
☐ Deodorant
☐ Detergent
☐ Insect repellent
☐ Lip balm
☐ Premoistened
   towelettes

☐ Sanitary pads/
   tampons
☐ Shampoo
☐ Shaver
☐ Soap
☐ Toilet paper
☐ Toothbrush
☐ Toothpaste
☐ Towel
☐ Water filter

Miscellaneous

☐ Address book
☐ Adhesive tape
☐ Bandanna
☐ Bicycle light
☐ Bungee cords (6)
☐ Compass
☐ Credit cards
☐ Dog repellent
☐ Driver's license
☐ Flashlight
☐ 10-inch hook-and-loop
   (like Velcro) straps
   (4)
☐ Lock
☐ Maps

☐ Money
☐ Notebook
☐ Nylon clothesline
☐ Nylon-mesh bag
☐ Pens (2)
☐ Plastic bags
☐ Quarters
☐ Safety pins
☐ Sewing kit
☐ Spare batteries
☐ State tourism packets
☐ Sunglasses
☐ Tape recorder
☐ Water bottles (3)

Part Three

THE EUROPEAN ADVENTURE

11

EVERY CYCLIST'S DREAM

You can never really call yourself a cyclist until you've toured Europe. Just as every baseball fan needs to visit Yankee Stadium and every writer needs to study Hemingway, each cyclist should experience the sport's venerable roots. If you doubt it, consider these impressions by Bicycling *editor (and veteran European bike traveler) Joe Kita.*

On a summer Sunday morning just outside Evian, France, I heard the whir of approaching bicycle wheels and felt a firm hand on my shoulder. Its owner smiled, nodded a "bonjour," and motioned toward the rest of his club. At first glance, they looked like my father's golfing buddies—weathered, gray-haired and loudly dressed. But their leg muscles were sculpted and their faces full of youthful enthusiasm. This weekly ride was their bit of Sunday reverence. As the church bells ring, the roads throughout Europe are filled with thousands like them—colorful caterpillar pacelines strung out across the landscape. For a while, I rode along—an apprentice to their sacred tradition.

On a crystalline August afternoon in the Swiss Alps, I struggled skyward, a serpent of switchbacks cast before me in a way that left nothing to even a merciful imagination.

My legs had already cramped once and my will was about to seize, but I heard a car approaching and my pride triggered one last surge of adrenalin. Then there was a beep and applause—yes applause—and three people leaning out the windows yelling, "Bravo! Bravo!" In Europe they know what it's like to challenge these mountains, and they respect all who try. For a few pedal strokes, I became LeMond on the final hairpin of L'Alpe d'Huez, and it felt great.

Amidst a dreary Monday morning rush hour on a bike path near Amsterdam, I saw a wrinkled old man of maybe 75 pedaling northward on a crinkled old bike. He had vegetables and flowers in his basket and a spotted white dog jogging behind. He didn't notice me. Despite my fancy helmet, jersey and bike, I was just another cyclist. In Europe, you blend in. At first it feels strange to no longer be an aberration, but then you slowly begin to realize the revelation in it all.

These are three important facets of cycling that you'll never experience riding your regular 25-mile training loop. Even a fall foliage tour in Vermont or a week-long cruise down the Pacific Coast Highway won't instill in you such a deep appreciation for what makes this sport so special. Surgeons say to feel a heart beating in your hand is to feel life itself. And the metaphor holds true for cycling. To ride with a grizzled group of French randonneurs, to climb the legendary mountains and hear even one "Allez!" and to lose yourself in a mass of Dutch bike commuters, is to feel the sport's heartbeat.

So go. Don't wait until you retire, or until you graduate, or until you can afford it. Make the time and borrow the money, because the longer you wait, the greater your chance of never going.

In fact, getting started is as easy as turning this page.

12 BICYCLING IN THE NEW EUROPE

The Berlin Wall has crumbled. The Iron Curtain is in tatters. But these aren't the only frontiers disappearing in Europe. With less fanfare, the borders between Western European nations are dissolving, too.

As trade barriers are lifted, the region is acting more like a single economic entity than a collection of nations. Certainly, national identities and cultural differences will always remain. But the countries of the European Community (EC) have become the world's largest single market.

To the locals, the changes have been known simply by the target date: " '92." And for cyclists, 1992 is good news. It makes traveling easier and less expensive in the EC countries of Belgium, Denmark, France, Greece, Ireland, Italy, Luxembourg, the Netherlands, Portugal, Spain, the United Kingdom and West Germany.

Some of the changes actually began before 1992. Across the region—in the EC countries as well as in Switzerland, Austria, Sweden, Norway, Iceland and Finland—1990 was designated the "European Year of Tourism." This was more than just a chamber-of-commerce campaign to increase business. In fact, it included substantial benefits for the European bike traveler. Among them were the introduction of discount air and rail passes and centralized European travel information. As you'll see, this was only the beginning of the positive changes bike tourists can expect in the new Europe.

Cycling Earns Some Recognition

Travel is already big business in Western Europe, employing 7.5 million people and accounting for nearly 6 percent of the region's gross domestic product. But the united Europe is focusing even more on tourism. "By the end of the century, it will be the most important industry on our continent," said EC commissioner Cardoso e Cunha.

A main emphasis is to attract Americans. The EC spends more than a million dollars annually in the United States on European travel promotion. And special deals, such as the discount air pass, are available only to non-Europeans.

Meanwhile, changes that directly affect cyclists are being made. Belgium hosted a major conference on cycling in the new Europe, with emphasis on how to develop safe new bike routes and coordinated tours across the continent. Organizers said the goal was to show policymakers the popularity of bike touring, and about 4,000 enthusiasts attended. Featured guests included Belgian prime minister Wilfried Martens and cycling great Eddy Merckx.

At a similar conference, EC transport minister Karl van Miert discussed the easing of customs formalities across Europe. The goal, he said, is "to increase the mobility of man." To make this happen, the united Europe will aim for safer roads and widespread bicycle access to buses and trains.

"We are trying to show that cycling is something to do for health, the environment and for the culture," says van Miert, himself a cyclist. He adds that bicycling is also one of the best ways to see the rural landscape and ancient towns of Europe.

Van Miert concedes, however, that these bicycle topics are not the EC's primary concern. He was more worried about the sticky issues of airline deregulation and pan-European transport policies. Until such problems are resolved, cycling concerns will be secondary.

In fact, some cycling issues are beyond EC control. Just as the United States leaves many questions to individual states, the united Europe is pushing for certain changes but letting each country control local issues.

Still, cyclists are benefiting. In coming years, the EC will have the power to implement widespread programs and improvements. It's likely that we'll see more trains with special cars to carry bikes, bike paths along new highways and in parks and cheaper fares for cyclists who use trains. Eventually, the EC may even assist in the creation of a mountain bike trail network, most likely in the Alps. In cities, the addition of secure bike parking facilities and new bike lanes also has EC support.

In addition, the growing environmental movement in Europe (the "green" movement) has been influencing EC leaders. Such sensitivity bodes well for cyclists. Part of the EC's environmental plan, for instance, includes promoting tourism in less-developed parts of the continent, away from the crowded big-city travel itinerary. But the EC recognizes that this must be done in a way that doesn't harm the back-country. That's why promoting rural bicycle travel is part of the plan. From an environmental standpoint, few tourists are as welcome as cyclists.

To attract bicyclists, the new Europe offers rail discounts to rural areas, as well as other incentives. In France, for example, a recently instituted plan gives cyclists a discount if they get off at one station and reboard at another.

Welcome Changes

All tourists to Europe can look forward to more convenience and less expense during their visits due to these developments.

Easier border crossings. When riding from one EC nation to another, you can expect a border crossing to be about as difficult as riding from Ohio to Indiana. Most likely, you won't have to show your passport or open your bags. Police won't board the trains. As frontiers dissolve, you won't even have to stop.

Cheaper flights. A discount air pass introduced in 1990 illustrates the new thinking. It was honored by a dozen airlines throughout Western Europe. You could buy 3,000 or 5,000 miles of air travel to be used within Western Europe during any two-month period. Unlike previous discount air passes, reservations could be made as late as 24 hours before departure. This made the new passes useful even when your schedule was uncertain. In addition, the price was competitive with the EurailPass, which also is offered only to non-Europeans. Such programs seem certain to continue.

Even without the pass, ticket prices fell as the national airlines lost their near-monopolies and cross-border competition began. The EC is pushing for a more competitive system in which airlines could fly anywhere in the community. Under the former system, only Italian and Spanish airlines could fly from Barcelona to Rome, for example. With deregulation, we'll see the same type of fare wars that have transformed U.S. flying.

All this makes a new type of European bike tour possible. Rather than pedaling from point to point or taking trains to cross long distances, it has become more practical to fly around the continent, using your bike (or a rental) to sample each destination's diverse culture, terrain and scenery.

Cheaper train travel. The tradition of seeing the continent by train still has a place in the new Europe. In fact, it became less expensive with the introduction of the Euro Domino Rail Pass. This works like a coupon, offering a 30 percent discount on regular first- and second-class prices. It's valid for a month, has no age restrictions and is good in all EC countries and throughout Scandinavia. You can purchase one at European train stations and from travel agents.

New lodging networks. Inn-to-inn cycling across national borders, already one of the delights of bike travel in Europe, is now easier. A Belgium-based travel organization, Eurorelais, has received EC funding to create a European network of inns and bed-and-breakfasts. This will work like many of the national inn-to-inn networks, where travelers can get route information from a central source and make reservations for an inn while at any of the others.

Meanwhile in Britain, the European Federation of Camping Site Organizations has received EC funds to provide more information about its specialty.

More and better information. Planning a Western European bike trip is more convenient than ever, thanks to greater availability of maps and tour information. Outside of Europe, the method is still to use national tourism offices. (See chapter 13.) In addition, consult the centralized travel sources listed on page 66. And once you're in Europe, check out the EC offices in major cities for pan-European travel information.

Easy money. The EC's financial services community is

standardizing automated teller machines throughout the continent. Before long, it should be possible to roll into Giverny, France, or San Gimignano, Italy, lean your bike against a wall, and use your credit or bank card to get a fistful of francs or lire.

New routes. With countries working together, imaginative bicycle routes are being devised. Soon you'll be able to trace the ancient paths of the Celts or Normans as they moved across Europe. Already, the Dutch and Belgian tourism federations have put together a tour called, "In the Track of Vincent van Gogh." As with almost everything else in the new Europe, the improvements are imminent and the possibilities staggering.

Recommended Maps

Unless you've got connections in the CIA, the kind of detailed maps you'll need for European bike touring can be difficult to find. The Michelin 900 series is excellent for planning a general route, as are the maps and guidebooks you'll receive from various tourist boards. But if you want to know whether a certain mile-long tunnel is lighted or what roads are under construction, you'll have to look elsewhere.

Once you're in the region you plan to tour, look for a blue sign bearing a white, lowercase "i." This will point you to the tourist office where you'll find the kind of advice and assistance you need. There are offices in even the smallest towns and villages, and they're also the best places to find locally operated and inexpensive accommodations.

Ask for maps in a scale of 1:100,000 (1 centimeter = 1 kilometer). These will show everything you need to know about road conditions, traffic, terrain, points of interest and the location of bike paths and scenic routes. If a map in this scale isn't available, settle for 1:200,000. It's a bit more vague, but it'll get you through. Anything above 1:300,000 isn't very useful for cyclists.

For more information about its resources (including dining guides), contact Michelin Guides and Maps, Box 5022, New Hyde Park, NY 11042.

Centralized Travel Sources

Other sources of information include:

- Alliance International du Tourisme, Quai Gustave Ador 2, 1207 Geneva, Switzerland; telephone 011-41-22-735-2727. Although primarily an automobile group, the alliance sponsors an annual weeklong summer bike rally in a rural European town. Events usually range upward from 20 kilometers.
- European Federation of Camping Site Organizations, c/o National Federation of Site Operators, 31 Park Rd., Gloucester FL1 1LK, Great Britain; telephone 011-44-4-522-6911. This organization is a clearinghouse for information about camping throughout Europe.
- European Travel Commission, 4 rue Linois, 75015 Paris, France; telephone 011-33-1-45-75-62-16. The ETC provides a wealth of European travel information, including a calendar of tourist events.
- Tourism Rural en Europe, 82 rue François Rolland, 94130 Nogent sur Marne, France; telephone 011-33-1-48-73-61-50 This group is helping to promote the new EC's emphasis on rural tourism. It provides information about small towns and villages that tourist agencies often miss.
- Federation des Auberges de Jeunesse de la CE, A.J. Parc du Rhin, rue des Cavaliers, 67000 Strasbourg, France; telephone 011-33-88-60-10-20. This is the European Youth Hostel network. In Europe there are many more hostels than in the United States, but they tend to be crowded during summer. American Youth Hostel cards are honored; nonmembers can get a free guest card at any hostel. (Nightly prices are a few dollars more for guests than for members.)

13 EURO TOUR PLANNER

Sit back and plan your European dream tour as we tell you where to find a great $10 dinner for two, the coziest bed-and-breakfasts, a place where cyclists are worshipped and much more.

Belgium

Plus: Excellent road system and flat-to-rolling terrain.

Minus: You can't use the excellent road system. If there's a bike path nearby you have to ride on it, no matter how crowded it is.

Out of the saddle: Trains are accessible and accommodating to bikes.

Weather: Humid and cloudy, with temperatures in the seventies from May to September. Fourteen days a month see some rain, and it's usually windy.

Cycling sight: Visit Meensel-Kiezegen, the birthplace of the legendary Eddy Merckx, five-time winner of the Tour de France.

Language: Primarily Flemish, but French is spoken in the south and English will get you by.

Cost: Moderate hotels, $75; campgrounds, $6; hostels, $4. Food prices are comparable to those in the United States.

Miscellaneous: Good, cheap beer.

Maps and more: Belgian Tourist Office, 745 5th Ave., New York, NY 10151 (212-758-8130).

Denmark

Plus: Flat terrain and a clearly marked network of bike paths make this an excellent spot for first-timers and families.

Prices and policies that were in effect when this chapter was written may have changed. Always check for current information.

Minus: The state-run railway (DSB) insists you bring your bike to the station one day before departure.

Out of the saddle: Most other trains allow bikes and have fewer restrictions. Ferries will take bikes anytime for a nominal fee.

Weather: June, July and August have average high temperatures in the seventies. Showers are most likely in the month of August, and stiff winds blow from the west.

Cycling sights: A bronze sculpture of a woman atop a building in Copenhagen's Town Hall Square serves as a weather forecaster. When she appears with an umbrella, expect rain, but if she's on her bike the weather will be fine. Rain or shine, mailmen make their rounds on official yellow bicycles.

Language: Officially it's Danish, but English is widely spoken.

Cost: Moderate hotels, $30 to $100; network of cottages and farmhouse rooms, $15 to $20; hostels, $5; campgrounds, $5. Lunch in an inexpensive restaurant is $8 to $10.

Miscellaneous: Bornholm, a resort island, has beautiful white beaches, quaint fishing villages and a forested nature reserve that's best toured by bike. The least-crowded time to visit is late August and September.

Maps and more: For general information: Scandinavian Tourist Boards, 655 3rd Ave., New York, NY 10017 (212-949-2333). For cycling information: Danish Cyclist Federation, Dansk Cyklist Forbund, Kjeld Langes Gade 14, 1367 Copenhagen K, Denmark (telephone 011-44212).

France

Plus: Excellent system of "D" (secondary) roads offering little traffic and great scenery. Gourmet food, wine and quaint lodging is easily accessible.

Minus: Snotty waiters who are offended by fractured French.

Out of the saddle: You can put your bike on a train, but it may arrive a day later than you if you transfer. If you

must change trains, buy individual tickets to each destination rather than one for the entire trip. Then at each station, claim your bike and take it to the next train.

Weather: From May through October the weather is
good for cycling in most of the country, with temperatures
in the seventies and eighties. The mountainous regions
have shorter, cooler summers, and the south stays warm
most of the year. The wine regions average 10 to 12 days
with some rain during the summer.

Cycling sights: The Tour de France consumes the
country for three weeks each July. Test your muscle by
riding some of the route or just watch the top pros race by.
Many memorials to famous cyclists are scattered throughout the country. A striking tribute stands near the summit
of Mont Ventoux in the province of Provence. Here, a statue
commemorates the spot where British racer Tom Simpson
collapsed and died during the 1967 Tour.

Language: Outside of tourist areas the natives find
amusement in hearing visitors struggle with French, but
English is generally understood.

Cost: City hotels, $75; hostels, $5; campgrounds, $4.

Miscellaneous: Get a good, cheap sleep in Gîtes
d'Étape, Gîtes de France or Chambres d'Hôte. Gîtes d'Étape
cost about the same as a hostel and have a bed and basic
cooking and washing facilities. Gîtes de France rent by the
week and provide all the comforts of home. Chambres
d'Hôte are similar to English bed-and-breakfasts—private
homes that provide a room and meal. Restaurant food is
expensive but worth it. Avoid places posting their menus
in English as well as French. You'll often pay more and get
less (quality and quantity).

Maps and more: France is among the world's top destinations for cycling vacations. Its tourist industry is accustomed to dealing with cyclists. For general information:
French Tourist Office, 610 5th Ave., New York, NY 10020
(212-757-1125). For lodging and reservation information on
the Gites, write for the "French Farm and Village Holiday
Guide," McCarta Ltd., 122 King's Cross Rd., London WC1X
9DS, England. The Cyclist's Touring Club (Cotterel House,
Surrey GU7 3HS, England) has detailed information and
maps for French touring.

Germany

Plus: A country your mother would love—clean and orderly.

Minus: The large U.S. military presence has soured some Germans on Americans.

Out of the saddle: Trains that carry baggage accept bikes for about $2; buses don't.

Weather: Cycling weather is best from May through October, with highs in the sixties and seventies. On average, 13 days of every month receive at least a trace of precipitation.

Cycling sight: Cologne hosts an exhibition of bikes and motorcycles (antiques to new models), usually in September.

Language: English is widely understood because it's taught as a second language.

Cost: Moderate hotels, $40; inns and bed-and-breakfast–type accommodations, $15 to $30; hostels, $7; campsites, $8. Dinner in an average restaurant is $12 to $25.

Miscellaneous: The Autobahn satiates the German need for speed, leaving country roads to slower, local traffic. However, motorists are used to driving fast and passing often, so beware.

Maps and more: For general information and reservations: German National Tourist Office, 630 5th Ave., New York, NY 10020 (212-308-3300).

Greece

Plus: Pedaling past ancient ruins that stretch your sense of time and history.

Minus: The tourist hordes, heat, dust and choking exhaust fumes of the summer vacation season. Secondary routes offer no escape. They're usually little more than farm paths—unpaved and covered with rocks and goat stuff.

Out of the saddle: Trains usually carry bikes for free. Arrive one hour before departure to check in. Buses in outlying areas supposedly accept bikes, but some hard-headed drivers refuse. Ferries transport bikes for a small fee.

Weather: Summers are hot and dry, with temperatures in the nineties during July and August. It's generally warm enough for year-round touring. Winter is considered the rainy season, but even then there are only five days of rain per month. Winds during spring and summer blow hard in the afternoon.

Cycling sight: While pedaling on terra firma, pay your respects to Poseidon, the god of the sea, at his white marble temple at Cape Sounion on the Saronic Gulf.

Language: Beware of Greek, which has its own alphabet. Some English is spoken in tourist areas and cities, but rarely in the countryside. Since signs and directions are likely to be printed in Greek, learn a few phrases so you can at least ask for help.

Cost: Moderate hotels, $30; hostels, $5; campgrounds, $4; dinner with wine, $15.

Miscellaneous: As in other Mediterranean countries, women are liable to get unwanted and exuberant attention from local men. Also, when flying in or out of the country, budget extra time for customs, then add two more hours to that. Security is tight in Greece.

Maps and more: For brochures and information: Greek National Tourist Organization, 645 5th Ave., New York, NY 10022 (212-421-5777).

Ireland

Plus: Misty green hills and winding country roads transport you back to a simpler time. Relax in a warm pub sipping Guinness with friendly red-cheeked (and sometimes red-nosed) local patrons.

Minus: Jumping every time you hear a loud noise in Northern Ireland.

Out of the saddle: Trains and buses accept bicycles.

Weather: Bring rain gear and expect cool temperatures. Highs in June, July and August are in the sixties and low seventies. Showers are likely at any time. June is usually the driest summer month.

Cycling sight: Ride the roads that nurtured native pro Sean Kelly in his hometown of Carrick-On-Suir.

Language: English is the official language, but natives may also speak Gaelic.

Cost: Hotels, $30; bed-and-breakfasts, $20; hostels, $5; campgrounds, $5. Dinner in a good restaurant is $15 to $20; pub food is less.

Miscellaneous: Traffic travels in the opposite direction. Be careful after taking a break because your natural inclination will put you on the wrong side of the road.

Maps and more: The Irish Tourist Board actively encourages bicycle touring by providing more comprehensive information for cyclists than any other country. For maps, do-it-yourself tour guides, bed-and-breakfast reservation information and hostel and campground guides: ITB, 757 3rd Ave., New York, NY 10017 (212-418-0800).

Italy

Plus: Eat your way across the country without guilt. This is the carbohydrate capital of the world.

Minus: Sharing long, unlighted tunnels in the mountains with the infamous native drivers in their flying Fiats.

Out of the saddle: Trains accept bikes as regular baggage. Buses are supposed to, but it often depends on the driver.

Weather: The south is extremely hot in summer, with temperatures in the nineties. December to February is the rainy season. Cycling is most pleasant in spring and fall, with highs in the sixties and seventies. The northern mountains are best in summer, with similar temperatures. During summer expect eight or nine rainy days in the north and two or three in the south.

Cycling sights: If racing is a religious experience for you, skip the Vatican and head for the chapel of the Madonna del Ghisallo in Megreglio, a tiny village in the mountains of northern Italy. Jerseys and caps worn by legends such as Fausto Coppi adorn the walls, medals and trophies are on display and bikes hang from on high. To see modern heroes, check out the Giro d'Italia, which spans three weeks beginning in mid May.

Language: In addition to Italian, English is spoken in

cities and tourist areas. German is common in the mountain districts, and French will get you through in a pinch.

Cost: Moderate hotels, $25; pensions and inns, $20; hostels, $4; campgrounds, $4. Groups can rent a cottage or farmhouse for about $20 per person. Food prices are about the same as in the United States.

Miscellaneous: You probably know that Vatican City is a sovereign state surrounded by Rome. Bet you didn't know that Italy also encloses the tiny republic of San Marino. Founded in A.D. 350, it's inland from the Adriatic, near the city of Rimini. It's one-tenth the size of New York City, and its major export is postage stamps.

Women cyclists can expect hassles from overly solicitous Italian men. Stores and restaurants close from about 1:00 to 4:00 P.M., so plan lunch stops accordingly.

Maps and more: For general information: Italian Government Travel Office, 690 Park Ave., New York, NY 10020 (212-245-4822).

Luxembourg

Plus: Boost your ego by riding across an entire country in one day.

Minus: A lot of people in such a little space means congestion.

Out of the saddle: Trains carry bikes as accompanied or unaccompanied luggage. With the former, you're expected to load and unload the bike. Space is limited, so try to arrive early, and there is a small fee. As unaccompanied luggage, the bike may arrive a day after you, and there's a slightly higher fee. Buses don't carry bicycles.

Weather: It's warm enough for comfortable riding from May through September, with highs in the sixties and seventies. Expect 10 to 12 days with some rain per month.

Cycling sights: Luxembourg is smaller than Rhode Island but has the densest concentration of castles per square mile of any country in Europe. There's one at the top of virtually every hill, making the effort worthwhile. Tours are offered at 17 castles, forts and medieval ruins.

Language: Officially French, but natives speak a dialect called Luxembourgeois, which only they understand. German is also spoken, and English is generally understood.

Cost: Moderate hotels, $75; inn, $35; boarding house, $15; hostel, $6. Dinner in a moderate restaurant costs $20.

Miscellaneous: Don't change your money into Luxembourg francs. Belgian francs are accepted in Luxembourg, but Luxembourg's currency can't be used elsewhere.

Maps and more: For general information: Luxembourg Tourist Office, 801 2nd Ave., New York, NY 10017 (212-370-9850).

The Netherlands

Plus: Everybody bicycles. An extensive network of paths takes you away from motor traffic.

Minus: Everybody bicycles. The paths are crowded and unmarked since the locals already know where they're going. These paths also have a tendency to end in the middle of nowhere.

Out of the saddle: Trains with baggage cars accept bikes for a fee. Space may be limited, so arrive early.

Weather: From May through September expect highs in the sixties and seventies. Rainfall is consistent throughout the year (14 to 15 days with some rain per month), with a little more from July to October. Wind constantly blows across the flat terrain.

Cycling sight: Head for the town of Kinderdijk, on the Lek River southeast of Rotterdam, for the highest concentration of working windmills in the country.

Language: Dutch is the official language, but many people speak English, especially the young.

Cost: Moderate hotels, $30; hostels, $8; about 70 campsites comprise the Sticting Gastvrije Fietscampings, $5. Dinner in a moderate restaurant is $15.

Miscellaneous: Because the bike paths can end unpredictably, don't try to keep a strict schedule. Just relax and dare to get lost.

Maps and more: For general information: Netherlands National Tourist Office, 576 5th Ave., New York, NY 10036

(212-370-7367). For campground information and booking forms: Sticting Gastvrije Fietscampings, Rijksstraatweg 117, 7231 AD Warnsveld, The Netherlands.

Portugal

Plus: The best touring value in Europe.

Minus: The rest of Europe knows. The coasts are packed during summer.

Out of the saddle: Public transportation isn't dependable outside of the major cities.

Weather: Summers are dry throughout the country. Temperatures are generally in the seventies and eighties from April through October.

Cycling sight: A big part of Portugal's charm is that it remains much as it has for centuries, especially in the interior Alentejo region.

Language: The native tongue is Portuguese, with little English spoken in major cities. A knowledge of Spanish or French is extremely helpful.

Cost: Government-run and privately owned guesthouses, $10 to $50; hostels, $3; campgrounds, $3. Dinner with wine, $5.

Miscellaneous: There are no hotels outside of the two major cities, Lisbon and Porto. So for a summer tour, reserve guesthouse space well in advance. As in Italy and Spain, shops and restaurants close during the hottest part of the day, usually from 1:00 to 3:00 P.M.

Maps and more: For general information: Portuguese National Tourist Office, 548 5th Ave., New York, NY 10036 (212-354-4403). For lodging information and reservations: Directorate General of Tourism, Av. Antonio Augusto de Aguaiar 86, Lisbon, Portugal.

Spain

Plus: Dinner for two (with wine), $14.

Minus: Those in the know say that the delicious tapas are made from songbird meat.

Out of the saddle: Trains with baggage cars transport bicycles; buses don't.

Weather: Temperatures in the south are in the upper nineties during July and August. The north is warm during summer, as well, although it can get quite cold at night in the higher elevations.

Cycling sight: In the Cantabria region on the northern coast, the Altimira Caves and the caves at Puente Viesgo are filled with beautifully preserved prehistoric wall paintings.

Language: Spanish is spoken, but with local peculiarities and more quickly than in your high school class. English is understood in the cities, less so in rural areas.

Cost: Moderate hotels, $20; hostels, $4; campgrounds, $5; guesthouses similar to bed-and-breakfasts, $15. The last is designed for motorists but works for cyclists as well.

Miscellaneous: Shops and restaurants close for a few hours in the early afternoon for siesta.

Maps and More: For brochures and reservations: National Tourist Office of Spain, 665 5th Ave., New York, NY 10022 (212-759-8822).

United Kingdom (England, Scotland, Wales)

Plus: The cozy bed-and-breakfasts and country inns are fit for a queen.

Minus: Food and weather are a royal pain.

Out of the saddle: Some trains allow bikes, others do not. Bikes aren't allowed on buses, but you can take them on passenger and car ferries. The roomy London taxis can easily transport you and your bike. Use them to escape the airport.

Weather: England is notoriously wet (16 days with rain per month), so bring rain gear and pack with plastic to keep things dry. From May through September temperatures are consistently mild, with highs in the sixties and seventies. Wales warms up later, with the best touring months being June, July and August. Scotland is also wet, stiff winds are common and it's colder, with summer highs in the low sixties.

Cycling sight: Hills steeper than you can believe. Install a very low gear or you'll be walking some of them.

Language: Communicating in English with the locals, especially in the rural areas, can be surprisingly difficult because of different accents and expressions. In Wales, Welsh is spoken along with English.

Cost: Moderate hotels, $75; bed-and-breakfasts, $20; hostels, $5; campgrounds, $4. Dinner in a moderate restaurant, $15.

Miscellaneous: To reserve a room in a bed-and-breakfast, go to the nearest tourist information center that is part of the Book-A-Bed-Ahead (BABA) network. Advance reservations by mail aren't accepted. There's no fee for the BABA service in Wales, but there is a small charge in England and Scotland.

Maps and more: General information: British Tourist Authority, 40 West 57th St., New York, NY 10019 (212-581-4700). Cycling information and maps: Cyclist's Touring Club, Cotterel House, 69 Meadrow, Godalming, Surrey GU7 3HS, England.

MOUNTAIN BIKE HEAVEN

Mountain bikes aren't just an American phenomenon. They're also the newest thing to hit the old country. In fact, they're being viewed as the best way to see Europe on two wheels.

Unlike in America, where it took the mountain bike years to reach the mainstream, Europe's fascination has been sudden and dramatic. If America had a mountain bike boom, then Europe is having an explosion. Some evidence:

- In 1987 there were 10,000 to 12,000 mountain bikes in England. By the end of 1990, there were 1.7 million. "Participation," says one British observer, "is increasing quadratically."
- Swiss ski resorts have begun renting mountain bikes and permitting them on lifts. During relatively snow-

less winters in recent years, mountain biking is credited with bolstering the industry.

- Europe's premier mountain bike race series (the Grundig World Cup) spans some ten countries. It's backed by big-name corporate sponsorship and typically draws up to 500 competitors and thousands of spectators. Smaller races are also becoming popular, with Germany hosting more than a hundred. In terms of talent, American racing experts concede that U.S. domination of the sport is over.

But beyond these impressive figures, the mountain bike is having a subtler yet even more dramatic effect. For bicycle travelers it's exposing a previously hidden Europe —one of wilderness, adventure and solitude that very few Americans have seen. The possibilities are endless and enticing. Since the countries are much older than ours, there are more dirt paths and trails to explore—all cherished remnants of civilizations past.

The best off-road routes are only now being discovered. In most German towns, for instance, just beyond the city limits you'll find the dirt roads that journey through the nation's essence. In England, you can ride parkland walking trails that until recently had been unknown to cyclists. And in the Alps, mountain paths are the new riding challenge.

These treasures, which have made mountain biking a European craze, can make your vacation unforgettable and fresh— even if you've toured Europe before.

"We have a strong tradition of cycling in Europe," says Tym Manley, editor of *Mountain Biking U.K.* magazine, "but the roads are crowded with cars and so it's become a pain to ride your bike from here to there. With mountain bikes, you can ride in all kinds of places. There's a sense of freedom."

Scaring Hikers off the Trails

This freedom, however, isn't guaranteed. Trail access, which is becoming a widespread and serious problem in the United States, is also becoming an issue in Europe. It appears that we're on the verge of seeing some areas become off-limits.

Because of Europe's dense population, large parks and wilderness areas are precious and crowded. Hikers aren't anxious to share them with vehicles of any kind. And in a familiar scenario, a bad first impression has turned many environmentalists against the sport.

"At first, there were some black sheep among mountain bikers, and they've hurt the image," says Uwe Geissler, editor of *Bike* magazine. "They were fascinated by the speed they could reach downhill, and they scared a lot of hikers, who then complained to newspapers. So the first reports were that mountain bikes terrorize the whole country, that all of them are devils scaring everybody and animals, too."

Switzerland has banned mountain bikes from a few trails in the Alps. And other countries are considering similar regulations. According to Manley, it's only a matter of months before some British paths become off limits, too.

Nonetheless, most trails will remain open. The access issue may alter mountain biking in Europe, but it won't destroy it. In fact, countries are already using mountain bikes to lure visitors. Belgium's official tourist guide, for example, lists shops where you can rent them. You can expect more off-road guides, maps and articles in coming months and years, once the best riding areas are identified. Soon, the typical European bike tour may take place on an all-terrain bike.

Europeans Take to Mountain Bikes

You can feel confident about using a mountain bike to see Europe. Its durability will help you survive the infamous cobblestones, and should a rock or stick crunch your derailleur, it's possible to find replacement parts in almost any bike shop.

You're also increasingly likely to discover mountain bike specialty shops. They seem to be springing up quickly in countries where the sport is most popular: England, West

Germany, France, Switzerland, Austria and Italy. In these shops, you'll see all the gear needed to customize a mountain bike for touring, including racks, panniers, bags, fenders and bar-end extensions for multiple hand positions. With triple chainrings and ultra-low gears, the drivetrain is already perfect for pedaling a load up steep hills.

In Europe, you'll be sharing the trail with a new breed of continental cyclist. They don't consider the mountain bike a diversion for when they tire of road riding. Rather, it's their primary bike. In fact, of 13,000 *Bike* readers surveyed, 68 percent don't own a road bike. The majority ride off-road (98 percent), and many use them for vacation exploration.

These enthusiasts ride mountain bikes for the same reasons Americans do. Sturdy frames, tough treads and an upright position are appealing whether you are from Peronne, France, or Peoria, Illinois.

"Certainly, mountain bikes with their bright colors and different look are sort of a fashion now," Geissler says. "But there's no question that they're more than that. They're a good idea. European cycling will never be the same."

15 WHEN YOU FLY AND YOUR BIKE FLIES WITH YOU

Traveling overseas with your bike can be a risky proposition. At the very least, your wallet may take a beating. At worst, your bike might. Fortunately, you can minimize the risk with some prudent planning.

The first thing to consider is whether you even need to take your bike. If you're planning a long, self-supported tour, it's best to use your own equipment. But if it's a more varied trip, perhaps taking trains throughout the continent and riding only in selected areas, consider renting. Most European bike shops offer rentals. They're simple-but-sturdy 3-speeds that are acceptable for short trips. By renting, you can travel unencumbered through airports and train stations. Renting is also a good idea if you're joining a commercial bike tour. Most companies offer good rental bikes at a reasonable cost.

If you decide to take your bike, make flight arrangements for your bike when you make your airline reservations. If you're working with a travel agent, stress that your bike's welfare is a priority.

Ask about extra travel insurance for your bike. By law, airlines only have to pay $9 per pound for lost luggage. That's about $360 for the average 40-pound boxed bike, far less than it may be worth. If your homeowner's or renter's insurance doesn't cover items lost or stolen while traveling, buy some extra coverage through your travel agent and purchase your tickets with an American Express, Carte Blanche or Diner's Club card. These companies offer supplemental coverage that will usually handle what the airline and insurance does not. Check with the bank issuing your card for its rules. (If you do a fair amount of traveling, it may be less expensive to buy a personal articles/all-perils policy giving you year-round protection.)

Most international airlines consider a bike to be part of your luggage allowance (two checked bags and one carry-on per passenger), but some draw the line at tandems. Most want the bike in a box or hardshell container; some accept it in a bag. There's little consistency among airlines in this area, and rules change constantly. You may even get conflicting stories from employees at the same airline. When calling, take notes and get the names of the people you speak with. Ask for a copy of the baggage policy, and take it with you to the airport. Then, if a dispute arises during check-in, show the agent this copy, as well as the names of the employees you spoke with. All this may seem like overkill, but it's still easier than a last-minute airport hassle.

Why Choosing the Container Matters So Much

The amount of disassembly that's required with your bike depends on the shipping container. Most people ask a local shop to pack their bike in one of the cardboard boxes that new bikes come in. This involves removing handlebar/ stem, saddle/seatpost, pedals and front wheel. (See chapter 16.) For extra protection, ask that the frame be wrapped in cardboard or a few layers of the plastic bubble wrap available at post offices.

Fill the box with as much gear as possible without making it too heavy. This will minimize the other luggage you have to carry (and possibly pay for) and further cushion the bike.

Comparatively, bike bags, generally made of thick canvas, require the most disassembly. Some models can be slung over a shoulder, but they usually aren't as protective. In fact, the types available from airlines are often nothing more than large garbage bags.

Hardshell cases are another, albeit more expensive, option. They offer the best protection, but you're faced with finding a place to store it until your flight home. Some airports (Shannon in Ireland, for example) provide storage space. But often, if you're using a box, the only alternative is to throw it away and hope you can obtain another later.

Whatever method you choose, make sure nothing protrudes and that it's obvious there's a bike inside. Put your name, address and phone number in various locations on the outside.

One technique is to establish a home base in a hotel near the airport. Spend the first and last night of your trip there. This gives you some place to leave your case or box and other bulky luggage. It also allows you to receive messages from home. This is especially important if you don't have a firm itinerary. Some cyclists go as far as asking the hotel concierge to call the U.S. embassy if they don't return on time. If you crisscross the area, you can leave belongings at the hotel and switch dirty clothes for clean halfway through the tour.

If you're using a home-base hotel, put its address and phone number on everything as well. You still might lose your luggage or bike (airlines being what they are), but at least you'll have a better chance of seeing it during your trip.

Finally, if you can't find your bike's original purchase receipt, have it appraised at a shop before leaving. In the unfortunate event that the airline does lose your bike forever, this estimate will help you get reimbursed more quickly.

16 BOXING A BIKE FOR SHIPMENT

Here's the step-by-step procedure for disassembling and boxing a bike for an airline flight or shipment via a parcel company. Often the latter is less expensive and more convenient (at least for domestic trips), since you don't have to travel with the bike in tow. However, you will be without it for several days while you send it ahead and await its return.

Here is what you'll need to disassemble and pack your bike:

- 5- and 6-mm allen wrenches
- Plastic mallet
- Small screwdriver
- Pliers
- 10-mm combination wrench
- 15-mm combination or pedal wrench
- Pipe insulation, bubble wrap or newspaper
- Fork spacer (available at shops) or a 100-mm-long block of wood
- Bike box (available at shops) of the correct width (for mountain or road bikes) and height (frame size is printed on the end)
- String
- Electrical tape
- Parts box (may be inside bike carton), shoe box or plastic bag
- Several stout rubber bands
- Packing tape (2-inch-wide filament or clear types)
- Black marker

Seven Simple Steps
to Guarantee Safe Shipment

Follow these guidelines for efficient disassembly and packing.

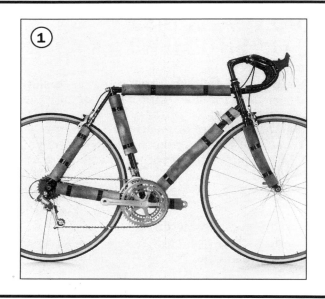

1.   Shift the chain onto the largest chainring and the second-largest cog. Remove the pedals (the left is reverse-threaded) and put them in the parts box or bag. To prevent damage, wrap each frame tube and the left crankarm with pipe insulation, bubble wrap or newspaper. Loosen the seatpost binder bolt and remove the seat and post together. Take off the bolt-on aero handlebar if you have one. Remove your cyclecomputer with its mount and unwind the wire from the brake cable. Individually wrap the seatpost, bolt-on bar and computer.
    2.   Loosen the bar and stem bolts with the allen wrenches. Tap the top of the stem bolt with the plastic

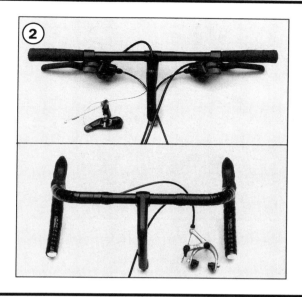

mallet to free the wedge or plug. Open both brake quick-releases or unhook cantilever brake transverse cables to create slack. On cantilevers with fixed transverse cables, use the 6-mm allen wrench to remove the cantilever that is attached to the main cable. This allows you to move the bar freely and position it in the box without disconnecting the cable. Keep the parts together with string or tape. Remove front sidepull brakes with a 5-mm allen or 10-mm combination wrench (don't disconnect the cable), then reattach the nut so it won't get lost. Wrap the unattached brake caliper or cantilever so it won't scratch the frame.

    3. Remove the front wheel. Unscrew the quick-release, reattach the springs and nut so they won't get lost, and put it in the parts box or bag. Install the fork spacer between the dropouts with screws or tape to prevent them from bending or penetrating the bottom of the box. Rotate the fork so it faces backward. Place the bike on the ground and level the crankarms. Move the valve stem between the seatstays and wrap a rubber band around it and the stays to keep the rear wheel from rotating.

4.   Place the front wheel on the left side of the bike.
Fit it as closely as possible by putting the left crankarm
between the spokes. This should allow the wheel to rest
against the frame with the axle above the down tube. Tie
the wheel against the down, seat and top tubes.

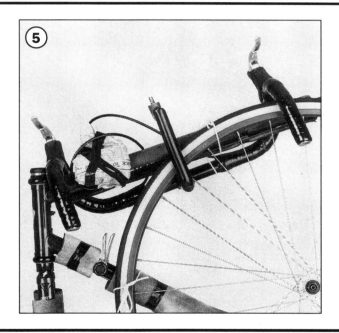

**5.   Place the bar/stem assembly over the top tube
and wheel.** Manipulate the stem to get it within the frame's
main triangle and make the package as narrow as possible.
Don't kink the rear brake cable.

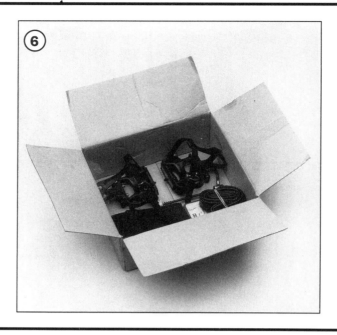

6.   Remove any staples in the box flaps with pliers so you won't get scratched. Check that all small items are inside the parts box or bag, tape it shut and place it toward one end of the bike carton.

7. Lower the bike into the box so that the small parts fit beneath the down tube. The bike's rear wheel and fork should rest on the bottom of the box. Move the bar/stem assembly so the flaps close and it doesn't create a bulge in the box. Insert the front brake wherever it fits. Place the seat/post assembly beside the rear wheel. Pack the bolt-on bar, a helmet or any other necessities where they'll fit. (All should be wrapped.) Close the flaps and tape the box shut. Add tape to the underside of the box for extra security. Use the black marker to cross out old addresses and add the correct ones.

Part Four
RIDING
TECHNIQUES

▮ 17 HANDLING A HEAVILY LOADED BIKE

Goodbye, daily grind. So long, schedules. There's something satisfying about leaving the bulk of your possessions behind and carrying all you need to live on a bike. But there are challenges, too. With as much as 50 extra pounds, your two-wheel Winnebago will handle dramatically differently. Here are some tips on setting up and piloting your home on the road. (Refer to the photo on page 92.)

1. Bike handling. You'll feel the increased weight (as much as 70 pounds for bike and baggage) in corners. Loaded bikes are more prone to sliding out in a turn, so go slower and lean less. Your training program should include some upper-body strengthening, as well as practice with a full load. It's also harder to accelerate and decelerate due to the increased mass, so avoid sudden starts and stops. When standing to pedal, keep the bike steady, rather than rocking it side to side. Also be sure to hold it upright when you stop at an intersection or walk with it, or it might tip out from under you.

2. Load distribution. The best arrangement is front and rear panniers. Opinions differ on weight distribution,

On a tour, your bike becomes your home away from home, but carrying lots of equipment presents some special challenges.

with some riders having best results with 60 percent of the load in back and 40 percent in front (for instance, 25/15 pounds rear/front). Others find the opposite to be better, so experiment. One thing is indisputable though: Weight should also be balanced left to right. Any type of front pannier arrangement is better than a heavily loaded handlebar bag, which can adversely affect steering. The best arrangement uses a low-mount rack that places the center of the panniers over the front axle. Some racks mount atop the wheel, but this puts the bags slightly higher and has a greater effect on handling.

3.   Frame. Your bike should provide a comfortable ride and be easy to control despite the added ballast. Look for relatively slack steering, including a 72- or 73-degree head angle and a fork with at least 2 inches of trail. Long, 17-inch chainstays will provide clearance between your heels and rear panniers and lessen the chain angles produced by the triple crankset. Tubing should be stiff and beefy to prevent wet-noodle handling in corners. For this reason, avoid conventional-diameter aluminum and carbon fiber. The ideal frame will also have threaded eyelets on the fork ends and rear dropouts, allowing you to securely attach racks and fenders.

4.   Brakes. Cantilever brakes are used on tandems because of their ability to handle more weight without losing stopping power. For the same reason, they're an excellent choice for a loaded touring bike. Also, new low-profile models eliminate the problem of interference with panniers. To improve stopping ability, stock brake pads can be replaced with aftermarket models that provide greater friction against the rim. These may also work better in the wet.

Always try to anticipate stops when carrying a load so you can maximize the stopping distance. You can apply the more powerful front brake hard, since the added weight in back means you're less likely to do an endo.

5.   Handlebar. For singletrack touring on a mountain bike, you'll need a flat bar for control. However, for fire roads and pavement, a drop bar's aerodynamic advantage will save you significant time and energy during a full day of riding. Also, by allowing you to support some body weight with your arms, it reduces saddle soreness—the bane of all tourists. Install a thick bar wrap to protect hands against vibration. An aero bar could be a tremendous boon in some situations, but practice beforehand to be sure you can handle the sensitive steering with a load.

6.   Packing. Experienced tourists know that whatever space you have, you'll fill. So don't buy the largest panniers unless you're sure you need them. (They range from 400 cubic inches per bag to about 2,000.) To improve handling, place the heaviest items low within the panniers. Lighter stuff that you'll need more often goes on top. Strap your sleeping bag and pad atop the rear rack, in line with the top tube. If you think it might rain, line the panniers with plastic garbage bags. Even the best coated models leak after a full day in the wet. Some riders like a small, easily removable handebar bag for their wallet and other frequently needed items. They carry it with them when they park the bike.

7. **Racks.** Today's light, welded aluminum racks are much stronger than the riveted, flexible models offered in the past. Some bikes have seatstay braze-ons that allow a more stable four-point mounting system rather than a three-point arrangement that uses the seatstay bridge. Secure the rack mounting bolts with thread adhesive. If your frame lacks eyelets, the Blackburn company makes clamps in various diameters for the fork and stays.

8. **Saddle.** A comfortable saddle can mean the difference between a successful tour and pure torture. Ride yours extensively beforehand to get used to its shape, keeping in mind that no saddle is comfortable all the time. (Use the riding tips in chapter 18 to maximize the time that it is.) A gel-padded saddle is favored by many tourists and almost always feels good initially, but some riders find that a firmer, foam-padded or all-leather model is a better friend down the road.

9. **Bottles.** Carry at least two bottles and drink frequently (about a bottle per hour). To obtain extra carbohydrate, mix water and fruit juice or use an energy drink. Some frames have braze-ons for a third bottle under the down tube near the bottom bracket. This low position is excellent for carrying a large-capacity emergency bottle (or stove fuel).

10. **Shoes and pedals.** If you've been using cleated shoes, you'll find it hard to forgo their power and efficiency on a tour. However, some people won't appreciate this fact as you clickety-clack your way across the floor of the Louvre. There are several options. You can use touring shoes (and toe clips) that have a sole designed for walking, or supplement your cleated shoes with a light pair of sneakers or sandals. Perhaps the best option is the new genera-

tion of clipless touring/off-road pedals and shoes. These boast a secure power link but use recessed cleats to enable quiet, comfortable walking. Models include Shimano Pedaling Dynamics (SPD), Look MX 90 and Time TWT.

11.   Wheels and tires. Since you can't effectively unweight a loaded bike over bumps, the wheels take much more abuse. The strongest option is a mountain bike's 26-inch-diameter wheels with wide tires. Pavement efficiency can be improved by installing slick or inverted-tread tires. To strengthen conventional 700C wheels, use at least 36 14-gauge spokes, wide 28C or 32C tires with a puncture-resistant Kevlar belt under the tread, and have a professional wheelbuilder assemble them. Inflate to the maximum recommended tire pressure (printed on the sidewall) to prevent pinch flats.

12.   Fenders. Lightweight fenders (also known as mudguards) help keep you drier and prevent gritty road water from fouling your brakes, drivetrain and panniers. Choose plastic rather than aluminum, which stays bent instead of springing back. Add reflective tape to the rear one as a safety measure.

13.   Gearing. A triple crankset's low gear is essential for loaded touring. If you'll be in mountainous terrain, have a granny gear of about 20 inches (e.g., 24-tooth smallest chainring paired with a 28-tooth largest cog). A high gear of 90 inches is sufficient, especially if you prefer to coast down most hills.

18 HIGH MILEAGE WITHOUT DISCOMFORT

As each day of a tour wears on, do you become more uncomfortable? Does your upper body get stiff, your neck sore? Do your hands grow numb? Does your saddle feel like it's turned into concrete? And do all of these things inhibit the strength of your lower body, making it harder to maintain the desired pace?

If the answers are yes, you're not alone, and you're probably blaming your bike. But before you banish it to a garage sale, try this: Put down the book for a minute and tense your shoulders so they're up near your ears. Then extend your arms in front of you and lock your elbows. Now clench your fists. Hold this position.

Uncomfortable, isn't it? Well, many people ride this way, and you may be among them. No wonder it's difficult completing 75 or 100 miles a day for a week or more.

Of course, the key to comfortable riding is a properly fitted bike. If you're uncertain about yours, visit a bike shop equipped with a Fit Kit or other professional sizing system. Then, after you're set up correctly, here are some things you can do to make long rides easier and more comfortable.

Tips for the Long Haul

Although your bike will never be an armchair, a high degree of comfort is attainable. If not, it wouldn't be possible for professional cyclists to race six to eight hours a day for weeks at a time, and events such as Race Across America would be inconceivable.

Pro cyclists prefer a long reach (distance from saddle to handlebar) and a relaxed frame geometry. A long reach, achieved by installing a long stem, helps keep their shoulders and back relaxed, while the shallower frame angles make for a smoother ride. Although such adaptations compromise responsiveness, they're crucial to riders who earn their living in the saddle. In general, touring cyclists benefit from a similar setup.

Court Comfort with Proper Clothing

For long-distance comfort, it's also essential to minimize the friction between you and the bike. It's the contact points—hands, feet, seat—that need the most attention.

Padded cycling gloves absorb road shock. But don't be fooled into thinking that all padding is the same. Many long-distance riders prefer gel over foam because it has the ability to move in any direction, thus preventing friction as it cushions. Choose gloves that also have an ample amount of soft, absorbent terry on the back, which is handy for wiping your eyes and nose.

Stiff-soled cycling shoes with cleats enhance pedaling efficiency and minimize foot fatigue. As mentioned in chapter 17, several companies make "walkable" models with recessed cleats, and these are ideal for touring.

Padded cycling shorts reduce friction in the crotch area. Buy a good-quality model with a soft, absorbent synthetic liner. In fact, buy two or three pairs so you'll always have a clean one to wear while the others are drying. If you feel self-conscious in skintight black Lycra, look for lined shorts cut more casually to resemble those made for walkers. Also new on the market are snug-fitting, padded Lycra shorts that resemble cut-off jeans, right down to their simulated zipper, pockets and seams.

Slight Bike Adjustments Pay Big Dividends

After your body is properly outfitted, check your bike. Even if you have a good overall fit, a few slight alterations can greatly enhance comfort.

First, your saddle must be adequate. If you're having trouble with it, make sure it's level and not excessively worn. Since there are subtle differences among saddles, experiment with various designs until you find one that feels good. But because no saddle stays comfortable all the time, help the situation by periodically standing to pedal even if there aren't hills that force you to. Just one minute off the saddle every half hour will relieve pressure, increase blood flow and provide cooling ventilation. This position change also helps stretch and relax the rest of your body.

Next, turn your attention to the handlebar. Some bikes come with bars that are 38-centimeters wide. But most average-size riders should have one that's 40 centimeters, and if you're big and broad shouldered, a 42-centimeter model will be even more comfortable.

In addition, the bottom tip of each brake lever should be aligned with the flat part of the handlebar drops (which, in turn, should be parallel to the ground or angled slightly downward toward the rear hub). Use a ruler to check this by holding it under each side of the bar and seeing if the lever tip touches. Such a position ensures optimum accessibility and comfort. Riding periodically with your hands atop the brake lever hoods will help keep your upper body relaxed.

While riding, keep in mind our stiff-shoulder experiment and how tiring it is to hold that position. Avoid grasping the handlebar in a death grip. With your palms on the bar, occasionally flutter your fingers. This will keep them light and relaxed but ready to steer and brake.

Keep your elbows unlocked as well. Riding with stiff arms is not only fatiguing but also dangerous because it severely limits your ability to make subtle changes in direction. Crashes often occur in races when people tense up and lock their arms. Try steering with your elbows locked, then relax them and feel the difference for yourself.

And get those shoulders out of your ears! Most cyclists ride this way simply because they don't realize they're doing it. Video-taping is an inexpensive and graphic way to notice such things. It's used extensively, for example, at the Carpenter/Phinney Cycling Camps at Copper Mountain, Colorado. All riders benefit from seeing themselves. Often it's the subtlest change in body position that yields the greatest results. But to make that all-important correction, you have to realize what you're doing wrong. The camera doesn't lie.

Change your position and/or riding style gradually, because sudden adjustments can cause injury. Reassess your progress periodically by video-taping or asking a training partner for his or her evaluation.

When you're on a long ride, think about your upper body as well as those strong, hard-working legs. Think of all the energy that a tense upper body wastes. Try to keep your back flat, and about once every half hour stand and arch forward to relieve low-back muscle tightness. Relax by taking a deep breath and completely exhaling all the tension. As you do this, drop your shoulders, unlock your elbows and flutter your fingers. For the long haul, you'll be happy you did.

■ 19 SAFE CYCLING IN WET WEATHER

If you're going to tour by bike, chances are very good that you'll find yourself riding in the rain at some point during the trip. If you have the right riding skills, equipment, clothing and mental outlook, rainy weather can be an interesting and challenging change of pace. Let's examine each of these important ingredients.

Traction Tips When Roads Are Slick

Since rain decreases traction, it's important to slow for corners to prevent sliding out, especially if you're on a heavy, loaded bike. When traffic permits, use a racer's trick and "straighten" the corner. To do this, approach the turn widely, gradually cut to the inside, then drift back out as you emerge from the corner. Some riders decrease the lean angle of the bike by moving their body over the top tube toward the inside of the turn. Others find it helpful to point their inside knee into the turn.

When climbing steep hills, and particularly when standing, your rear wheel may slip. Try using a lower gear while sitting, or shift your weight over the rear wheel when standing.

Even the best brakes become less effective in wet weather. Typically, there's a delay as the pads wipe water from the rims. Sand or mud worsens this. Test your brakes early in the ride to remind yourself of the increased stopping distance that's required. During long descents, maintain a slight drag on the rims to keep them free of excess water and allow quicker stopping.

Apply the brakes before a corner, rather than in it, to prevent locking the wheels and sliding out. Always favor the rear brake in the rain because it's much easier to control a skidding rear wheel than a front one. (Practice a rear-wheel skid on a straightaway to become accustomed to it.)

Pedaling through corners can help maintain tire adhesion. Brake before (not during) the crossing of hazardous surfaces such as those covered with leaves or gravel.

Surface oil can also decrease traction. Use extra caution during the first few minutes of rain, which serves to loosen the slippery film before washing it away. On a straight road, position yourself in the right wheel track to avoid the oil and make yourself visible to motorists.

Metal and painted surfaces are particularly hazardous. Be wary of rain grates, manhole covers, steel plates over excavations, expansion joints, grated bridges and all types of lane markings. Cross railroad tracks at a right angle.

And do as your mother told you and don't play in the puddles. It's not uncommon to find a gaping hole underneath. Look behind for traffic, then swing wide of standing water.

Storm Gear for Your Bike

When riding in the rain, much of the water and dirt that strikes you comes from your own wheels. That's why, if you plan to be an all-weather tourist, you should use fenders. These are common in Europe but are seen less frequently in the United States (except, perhaps, in Seattle). Not only will they help keep you and your panniers drier and cleaner, but they'll also make you popular with those behind because you won't send up a "rooster tail." Lightweight plastic fenders are available in various widths; wider is better than narrower for touring bikes.

The wider, treaded tires ideal for touring are also best for rainy roads. Some riders increase traction by decreasing air pressure about ten psi when rain begins. (If you do this, be careful of impact punctures.) Ironically, flats seem to occur more often in the rain, adding insult to injury. Be sure to carry a spare tube as well as a tire repair kit, since patches are difficult to apply in the wet.

If you anticipate riding in the rain often, you may want to invest in a sealed-bearing bottom bracket or hubs. These help prevent water from entering. Generally, cartridge types offer more water resistance than those using simple contact seals or "O" rings. Wet-weather riding also washes most of the lubricant from a chain, so be sure to add some afterward.

Your Wet Weather Wardrobe Is Important

Proper clothing can mean the difference between a pleasant (or at least tolerable) day in the rain and a miserable one. An essential element is a breathable, waterproof jacket made of a fabric such as Gore-Tex, 3M Thintech or Toray Entrant. Ideally, it should be a garment made for cycling. This means it is cut to the shape of a bent-over rider, has an extended rain flap over the buttocks, provides ventilation with vents on the back or under the arms (more effective) and is brightly colored and trimmed in reflective material.

Other items depend on the temperature. When it's cold, combine the rain jacket with one or two polypropylene or wool undershirts. It's important to have one of these wicking fabrics against your skin to help keep it dry. Other cold- and wet-weather items include insulated gloves, tights and shoe covers. (The most effective are made of neoprene or covered in a waterproof fabric.) Wool or polypropylene socks will keep your feet warm even when wet.

A cotton or wool cap takes up little space and provides additional warmth, and the bill helps afford a clear view. (You may need to remove a pad or two from your helmet to use one.) Alternatively, you can stretch a waterproof cover over your helmet to keep out water and hold in heat.

Use Your Brain When It Rains

Of course, even with the best clothing and equipment, you can't stay warm and dry indefinitely. (In fact, you may find you get as wet from sweat as from rain after a while.) This is part of cycling, and it's what makes traveling by bike an experience that not everyone can handle.

But as veteran travelers know, you can't do anything about the rain, so you might as well stop complaining about it. If feasible, shorten the day's mileage or even let the foul weather mandate a rest day. But if you must press on, you'll probably find that the rainy ride isn't nearly as uncomfortable as you imagine. Once you're out and pedaling, you'll see and hear a different world that's beautiful in its own right.

At the end of the day, use a hose or bucket to wash your bike (preferably while it's still wet). Be careful not to spray or pour directly at the bearings, then wipe it dry. Do the same for yourself, and take pride in the fact that you persevered. The sun will shine tomorrow.

20 HIGH-ALTITUDE CYCLING

Everyone who's ridden the Rockies knows the delights of high-altitude cycling—spectacular scenery and challenging terrain. But sea-level riders who head for the mountains also experience another revelation: Their fitness literally vanishes into thin air.

If you plan to be ridin' high on a bike tour sometime soon, take time to scan these tips on pedaling at altitude. They'll help you adapt quicker, recover faster and avoid such nasty side effects as headache, nausea and insomnia.

First, though, some background on the high ground. The reason it's harder to breathe at altitude isn't that there's less oxygen in the air. Rather, there's less barometric pressure forcing air into your lungs. To deliver enough oxygenated blood to working muscles, you must breathe faster and your heart has to pump more rapidly.

If you live near sea level, you probably won't notice any difference until you ascend above 5,000 feet. Studies of elite athletes show a significant 6 to 8 percent decrease in oxygen uptake at about 6,000 feet, according to Jay T. Kearney, Ph.D., director of sports science for the U.S. Olympic Committee. And at about 8,000 feet, you should be wary of acute mountain sickness (AMS).

What Happens When You're High Up?

The symptoms of AMS include headache, shortness of breath when exercising, insomnia, fatigue, irritability, decreased appetite, nausea and vomiting. These can appear as soon as four to six hours after reaching 8,000 feet. They're most severe on the second and third days and usually disappear by the fourth day. The only sure cure is to descend, although mild symptoms can be treated by going to bed and drinking lots of fluid.

Ironically, you're more likely to get AMS than a sedentary person. "The more fit you are, the more susceptible you are because you tend to push yourself harder," says Edmund Burke, Ph.D., an exercise physiologist in Colorado Springs (elevation: 6,000 feet).

Supporting his assertion is a study of U.S. Cycling Federation members competing in races held above 5,000 feet. Researchers found that 25 percent of the 1,500 riders had signs of AMS, although only 3.4 percent suffered moderate rather than mild cases.

The best way to prepare for high-elevation cycling is to make your body as efficient as possible by training harder than you would for a similar tour at sea level.

"A lot of people come to Fat Tire Bike Week thinking they're fit, but they find out they're not," says Don Cook, a former off-road racer who lives at 8,900 feet in Crested Butte, Colorado, home of the annual week-long festival that features all-day rides on a spectacular network of single-track. "You need to get in a lot of good, solid climbing miles and do some anaerobic stuff."

What You Can Do to Get Ready

Even if you're not a superpowered cyclist, though, you can perform well and stay healthy by getting reasonably fit and planning your trip carefully. Dr. Kearney says ideally you should have 10 to 14 days to acclimatize. The classic way is to ascend gradually, spending a day or more at intermediate altitudes. If you're going to tour Colorado, for

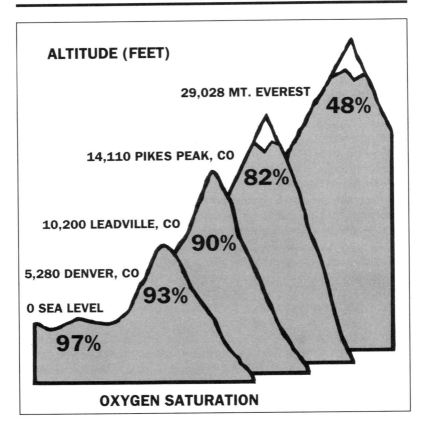

Percentage of oxygen in the blood at various altitudes.

instance, you might fly into Denver and spend a couple days in the mile-high city before climbing to a 1½-mile-high destination. If you're going even higher, to between 10,000 and 14,000 feet, experts recommend ascending 1,000 feet per day.

But don't despair if you haven't enough time to slowly acclimatize. Experts such as Dr. Kearney also say you can perform well with a blitzkrieg approach—doing your hardest riding as soon as you arrive at altitude. This can work if you're focusing on a weekend tour of two or three days.

"There are all sorts of opinions," says Cook, "but I know from experience that people who come up here are better off getting in their licks during the first few days." That's because it takes as long as 48 hours before the effects of altitude take hold, explains Dr. Burke.

After going hard initially, Cook recommends resting on the third or fourth day as your body adapts. "When my buddies come up from California, they're at their best the first couple of days," Cook explains. "Then all of a sudden they're walking up stairs, and it hits them."

After six or seven days, you're likely to experience a rally. If you're fortunate enough to be on a two-week vacation, you'll probably start feeling strong the last few days.

Dr. Kearney says this process is similar to what your body encounters in training. Like hard riding, pedaling at altitude is exhaustive and debilitating in the short term, but with proper recovery you get stronger.

To truly be on par with cyclists who live at altitude, though, you need to spend more time there. The reason is that it takes a while for your body to enhance its number of oxygen-carrying red blood cells. "There's this continual process of adaptation—of red blood cells increasing—and that requires many months," says Dr. Burke.

Rules upon Arrival at Altitude

Make it easier for yourself when traveling to high altitudes by following this worthwhile advice.

Don't take chances. If you experience AMS symptoms, stop riding. If they're severe, drop to a lower altitude.

Don't drink much alcohol. Not only will it (and coffee and soda with caffeine) further dehydrate you by increasing urination, says Burke, but "alcoholic beverages have roughly twice the effect at elevation than at sea level." This may sound like fun when you're hanging out at the bar in the evening, but it's not so enjoyable when you're hanging over the 'bar the next morning.

Eat more carbo, less protein. "A general carbodydrate diet and a decrease in the amount of protein ingested will lighten the load on your body as it works to restore a comfortable physiological balance," says Dr. Burke. Why? You can store more fluid in your body with carbohydrate, and it takes less oxygen to burn carbo at altitude.

Ride high, sleep low. If you have trouble sleeping at altitude, try to spend the night at a lower elevation than where you're riding. A drop of as little as 1,000 feet can be enough to help you breathe easier.

Block the sun. Solar radiation is greater at elevation, so wear sunscreen, sunglasses and light-colored clothing. If possible, avoid riding between 10:00 A.M. and 2:00 P.M.

Dress smart. The weather can change swiftly in the mountains, so take warm, water-repellent clothing to ward off hypothermia. And remember that for every 1,000 feet you ascend, the temperature drops about three degrees.

Drink lots of water. The air is drier at altitude, so you dehydrate quicker. Sweat also evaporates faster, making it harder to tell you're losing water. Drink plentifully while riding, and don't stop when you're off the bike.

■ A GUIDE TO BIKE TOUR COMPANIES

Here is an alphabetical listing of companies providing supported tours for cyclists. We regret that due to the diversity of locations served by various companies, we were not able to group companies by states, regions or countries. Most companies offer a brochure, so write or call for more information about areas served, support provided, costs and so forth.

Adrift Adventures, Box 577, Moab, UT 84532; phone: (800) 874-4483

The Adventure Traveller, Compston Rd., Ambleside, Cumbria LA2 9DJ, England

Alaska Bicycle Tours, Box 829, Haines, AK 99827; phone: (907) 766-2869 (Alaska; British Columbia, Yukon)

Alaska Travel Alternatives, Box 872247, Wasilla, AK 99687

All-Outdoors Adventure Trips, 2151 San Miguel Dr., Walnut Creek, CA 94596; phone: (415) 932-8993

American Lung Association of Michigan, 403 Seymore Ave., Lansing, MI 48933; phone: (517) 484-4541 (Michigan; Holland, New Zealand, Siberia)

American Wilderness Experience, Box 1486, Boulder, CO 80306; phone: (800) 444-0099 (Colorado, Montana, Utah, Wyoming; British Columbia)

American Youth Hostels of Delaware Valley, 38 S. 3rd St., Philadelphia, PA 19107; phone: (215) 925-6005

American Youth Hostels of New York, 891 Amsterdam Ave., New York, NY 10025; phone: (212) 932-2300 (northeastern United States)

American Youth Hostels of Ozark Area, 7187 Manchester, St. Louis, MO 63143; phone: (314) 644-4660 (Illinois, Missouri)

American Youth Hostels of Washington State, 419 Queen Anne Ave. N., #108, Seattle, WA 98109; phone: (206) 281-7306

Appalachian Valley Bicycle Touring, Box 27079, Baltimore, MD 21230; phone: (410) 837-8068 (Maryland, Pennsylvania, West Virginia)

Atlantic Canada Bicycle Rally, Box 1555, Station M, Halifax, Nova Scotia, Canada B3J 2Y3; phone: (902) 469-1253 (New Brunswick, Nova Scotia, Prince Edward Island)

The Ausen B&B, RR 2, Didsbury, Alberta, Canada T0M 0W0; phone: (403) 335-4736 (Alberta)

Australian Outbike Tours, 1972 Lascanoas, Santa Barbara, CA 93105

Backcountry Bicycle Tours, Box 4029, Bozeman, MT 59772; phone: (406) 586-3556 (Colorado, Montana, New Mexico, Washington, Wyoming; Canadian Rockies)

Backroads, 1516 5th St., Suite LD, Berkeley, CA 94710; phone: (800) BIKETRIP (Asia, Central America, Europe, North America, the Pacific)

Baja Expeditions, Inc., 2625 Garnet Ave., San Diego, CA 92109; phone: (619) 581-3311

Bay Area Biking, Box 6264, Carmel, CA 93921; phone: (403) 647-8917 (California)

Bicycle Adventure Club #1, 3904 Groton St., San Diego, CA 92110; phone: (619) 226-2175 (Arizona, California, Colorado, Hawaii, Iowa, Montana, New Mexico, New York, Ohio, Utah; Bali, Canada, France, Germany, Italy, Netherlands, New Zealand)

Bicycle Adventures, Box 7875, Olympia, WA 98507; phone: (206) 786-0989

Bicycle Africa, 4887-L Columbia Dr., South Seattle, WA 98108; phone: (206) 628-9314

Bicycle Beano Vegetarian Tours, Brynderwen, Erwood Builth Wells, Powys LD2 3PQ, England (England, Wales)

Bicycle Tour Services, Box 11-296, Auckland 5, New Zealand (New Zealand)

Bike & Cruise, 10250 SW Greensburg Rd., Portland, OR 97223

Bike Arizona, 7454 E. Broadway #102, Tucson, AZ 85710; phone: (602) 722-3228

Bike California, American Lung Association, 917 3rd St. Davis, CA 95616; phone: (800) 827-2453 (California)

Bikecentennial, Box 8308-L1, Missoula, MT 59807; phone: (406) 721-1776 (Canada, United States)

Bike Holland, 1755 Deweese St., Fort Collins, CO 80526; phone: (303) 226-3645

Bike Quest, Box 332-TF, Brookdale, CA 95007; phone: (408) 338-2477

Bike Riders, Inc., Box 254, Boston, MA 02113; phone: (800) 473-7040 (Massachusetts, Rhode Island; Greece, Italy)

Bike the Whites, Box 189, Tamworth, NH 03886; phone: (800) 933-3902 (New Hampshire)

Bike Tour France, 5523 Wedgewood Dr., Charlotte, NC 28209; phone: (704) 527-0955 (France)

Bike Tours, Box 75, Bath, Avon BA1 1BX, England (China, Denmark, England, France, Holland, Ireland, Italy, Kenya, Spain, United States)

Bike Vermont, Box 207-L, Woodstock, VT 05091; phone: (800) 257-2226 (Vermont)

Bon Voyage Specialty Tours, 825 S. Shields, Ft. Collins, CO 80521; phone: (303) 493-8511 (China, Europe)

Breakaway Vacations, 164 E. 90th St. #2Y, New York, NY 10128; phone: (212) 722-4221

Breaking Away Bicycle Tours, 1142 Manhattan Ave., Suite 253, Manhattan Beach, CA 90266; phone: (213) 545-5118 (Canada, Europe, United States)

Brooks Country Cycling & Hiking, 140 West 83rd St., New York, NY 10024; phone: (212) 874-5151

Bucks County Biking, Box 534, New Hope, PA 19838; phone: (215) 862-0733

Butterfield & Robinson, 70 Bond St. #300, Toronto, Ontario, Canada M5B 1X3; phone: (800) 387-1147 (Austria, Denmark, Germany, Hungary, Indonesia, Italy, New Zealand, Spain, United States)

Canusa Cycle Tours, 192 Elma St. #2, Okotoks, Alberta, Canada T0L 1T3; phone: (403) 938-5999 (Alberta, British Columbia; Montana, United States Rockies and coastal mountains)

Cape Cod Connection, 259 Main St., Hyannis, MA 02601

Cape Cod Cycle Tours, Box 1356, North Eastham, MA 02651; phone: (508) 255-8281 (Massachusetts)

Carolina Cycle Tours, Nantahala Outdoor Center, 41 US19W, Bryson City, NC 28713; phone: (704) 488-6737 (southeastern United States; Costa Rica, England, Scotland)

Champion Travel, PK 409, Kadikoy-Istanbul, Turkey (Turkey)

Chateaux Bike Tours, Box 5706, Denver, CO 80217; phone: (303) 393-6910 (France, Italy, Switzerland)

China Advocates, 1635 Irving St., San Francisco, CA 9412; phone: (800) 333-6474

Christian Adventures, 25 East 8th St., Holland, MI 49423; phone: (616) 392-9922 (Alaska, Arizona, Florida, Michigan, New Hampshire, Utah, Vermont, Wisconsin, Wyoming; Canadian Rockies, Nova Scotia)

Ciclismo Classico, Box 2405, Cambridge, MA 02238; phone: (617) 628-7314 (Italy, Spain)

Classic Bicycle Tours and Treks, Box 668, Clarkson, NY 14430; phone: (716) 637-5970 (Alabama, Mississippi, New York, Tennessee, Virginia; Nova Scotia, Prince Edward Island; England, France, Germany, Greece, Holland, Scotland)

College Bicycle Tours, 415 Fullerton Pkwy. #1003, Chicago, IL 60614

Colorado Heart Cycle Association, Box 100743, Denver, CO 80210; phone: (303) 278-1359 (Arizona, Arkansas, California, Colorado, Mississippi, New Mexico, Utah, Washington, Wyoming; British Columbia, Canadian Rockies; France, Switzerland)

Country Inns along the Trail, RR 3, Box 3115, Brandon, VT 05733; phone: (802) 247-3300 (Vermont)

Covered Bridge Bicycle Tours Plus, Box 693, Main Post Office, St. John, New Brunswick, Canada E2L 4B3; phone: (506) 849-9028 (Bay of Fundy, New Brunswick, Nova Scotia)

Coyote Bicycle Tours, Box 1832, Austin, TX 78701; phone: (512) 474-2714

Crocodile Cycles, Box 1486, Boulder, CO 80306; phone: (800) 444-0099 (Australia, New Zealand)

Cruiser Bob's Downhill Bicycle Tours, 99 Hana Hwy., Box B, Paia, HI 96779; phone: (800) 654-7717 (Hawaii)

Cycle America, Box 29, Northfield, MN 55057; phone: (800) 245-3263 (Arizona, California, Colorado, Maine, Michigan, Minnesota, Montana, New Hampshire, New York, North Dakota, Ohio, Oregon, Pennsylvania, Utah, Vermont, Washington, Wisconsin, Wyoming; Canada)

Cycle Inn Vermont, Box 243, Lidlow, VT 05149; phone: (802) 228-8799 (Vermont)

Cycle Path for Peace–Iowa, 209 East 13th St., Davenport, IA 52803

Cycle Swiss Alpine, Box 2216, Winchester, VA 22601; phone: (703) 662-1510 (Switzerland)

Cycleventures, 2517 Wilhaven Dr., Cumberland, Ontario, Canada K0A 1S0; phone: (613) 833-3343 (Canada, Europe, United States)

Cycle West, 75 Bush St., Ashland, OR 97520; phone: (800) 831-5016 (California, Oregon, San Juan Islands)

Cycling Arizona, 4466 E. Haven Ln., Tucson, AZ 85712; phone: (602) 322-0984 (Arizona)

Cycling through the Centuries, Box 877, San Antonio, FL 33576; phone: (800) 245-4226 (Denmark, England, France, Portugal, Spain)

Down East Tours, Comp. 41, RR 2, Kingston, Nova Scotia, Canada B0P 1R0; phone: (902) 765-8923

Earthventures, 2625 N. Meridian St., Suite 612, Indianapolis, IN 46208; phone: (800) 447-2866 (Kentucky; Australia, Austria, England, France, Italy)

Easy Rider Tours, Box 1384, Arlington, MA 02174; phone: (800) 488-8332 (New England, Pacific Northwest; Nova Scotia, Prince Edward Island; Ireland, Portugal, Portuguese Azores)

The 1860 House, Box 276, Stowe, VT 05672; phone: (800) 248-1860 (Vermont)

Elk River Touring Center, Highway 219, Slatyfork, WV 26291; phone: (304) 572-3771 (Virginia, West Virginia)

Embassy Cruise, Box 309, Keaau, HI 96749; phone: (808) 966-7907 (Fiji Islands, France)

Encompass Cycling Vacations, Box 3461, Madison, WI 53704; phone: (608) 249-4490 (Colorado, Florida, Kentucky, Louisiana, Michigan, Minnesota, Mississippi, New Mexico, Wisconsin)

Endless Summer Tours, 1101 Franklin, Michigan City, IN 46360; phone: (800) 345-3389

Euro-Bike Tours, Box 990, De Kalb, IL 60115; phone: (800) 321-6060 (Europe)

EuroEast Tours, 2247 Minor Ave., East Seattle, WA 98102; phone: (206) 522-0283 (eastern Europe, Russia, former USSR)

Europeds, 761 Lighthouse Ave., Monterey, CA 93940; phone: (800) 321-9552 (France, Switzerland)

Excursions Extraordinaires, Box 3493, Eugene, OR 97403; phone: (800) 678-2252 (Cascade Mountains, Oregon, San Juan Islands)

Explorations in Travel, Inc., 275 Jacksonville Stage Rd., Brattleboro, VT 05301; phone: (802) 257-0152 (New England; Europe)

Finger Lakes Cycling Adventures, Box 457, Fairport, NY 14450; phone: (716) 377-9817 (New York)

First American Bicycle Tours, 303 E. Southern #108, Mesa, AZ 85210

Forum Travel International, 91 Gregory Ln. #21, Pleasant Hill, CA 94523; phone: (415) 671-2900 (western United States; western Canada; Austria, Bali, Costa Rica, Czechoslovakia, France, Germany, Hungary, Ireland, Peru, Scotland)

Freewheeling Adventures, Inc., RR 1, Boutilier's Point, Nova Scotia, Canada B0J 1G0; phone: (902) 826-2437 (Newfoundland, Nova Scotia, Prince Edward Island; Scotland)

French Louisiana Bike Tours, 601 Pinhook Rd., East Lafayette, LA 70501; phone: (800) 346-7989 (Louisiana, Mississippi)

Fresco Cycling Holidays, 575 Pierce St. #303, San Francisco, CA 94118; phone: (415) 386-8266 (Lake Bolsena; Italy, southern Tuscany)

Gerhard's Bicycle Odysseys, Box 757, Portland, OR 97207; phone: (503) 223-2402 (Europe)

Goulash Tours, Inc., Box 2972, Kalamazoo, MI 49003; phone: (616) 349-8817 (Austria, Balkans, Baltics, Bulgaria, Czechoslovakia, eastern Europe, Estonia, Hungary, Latvia, Lithuania, Poland, Romania, Russia, Ukraine)

Grand Bicycle Tours, Box 37, Suite 2, RR 1, Elora, Ontario, Canada N0B 1S0 (Canada)

Hawaiian Pedals, 75-5744 Alii Dr., Kailua-Kona, HI 96740; phone: (808) 329-2294 (Hawaii)

Hawk Mountain Inn Cycle Tours, RR 1, Box 186, Kempton, PA 19529; phone: (215) 756-4224 (Blue Mountains, Pennsylvania)

Heartland Bicycle Tours, 1 Orchard Circle, Washington, IA 52353; phone: (319) 653-2277 (Iowa; Bahamas)

Heart of England Bicycle Tours, 2 Victoria Terr., Walsall, Westmidlands WS4 2DA, England

Hiking and Biking Scotland, Bogfur, Inverurie, Aberdeen AB5 9NT, Scotland

Hosteling International, Box 37613, Washington, DC 20013; phone: (202) 783-6161 (Canada, Europe, United States)

Imagine Tours RES Association, 917 3rd St., Suite E, Davis, CA 95616; phone: (800) 228-7041 (west coast of United States; Canada)

International Bicycle Touring Society, Box 6979, San Diego, CA 92106; phone: (619) 226-TOUR

International Bicycle Tours, 7 Champlin Sq., Box 754, Essex, CT 06426; phone: (203) 767-7005 (Florida, Massachusetts; Austria, England, France, Holland)

Island Bicycle Adventures, Box 458, Volcano Village, HI 96785; phone: (800) 233-2226 (Hawaii)

Israel Seminars Foundation, 110 E. 59th St., 3rd Fl., New York, NY 10022; phone: (212) 935-3578 (Egypt, Israel)

Italian Cycling Center, 2117 Green St., Philadelphia, PA 19130; phone: (215) 232-6772 (northern Italy)

Italia Velo Sport, 2724 Marty Way, Sacramento, CA 95818; phone: (510) 839-1744 (Italy)

Journeys Beyond, Box 7511-BG, Jackson, WY 83001; phone: (307) 733-9615

Kaibab Mountain Bike Tours, Box 339, Moab, UT 84532; phone: (801) 259-7423 (Arizona, Colorado, Utah)

Kolotour, Box 1493, Boulder Creek, CA 95006; phone: (408) 338-2979 (Czechoslovakia)

Ko'Olau Ridge Riders, 67-395 Garrington Hwy., Waialua, HI 96791 phone: (808) 637-6488

Kootenay Mountain Bike Tours, Ltd., Box 867, Nelson, British Columbia, Canada V1L 6A5; phone: (604) 354-4371

Lancaster Bicycle Touring, 3 Colt Ridge Ln., Strasburg, PA 17579; phone: (717) 396-0456 (Pennsylvania)

LeTour Bicycling Adventures, 1030 Merced St., Berkeley, CA 94707; phone: (800) 542-4210 (Australia, France, Holland, Italy, Switzerland)

Le Vieux Moulin, Box 4454, Vail, CO 81658; phone: (303) 476-1389 (France)

Lost World Adventures, 1189 Autumn Ridge Dr., Marietta, GA 30066; phone: (800) 999-0558 (Costa Rica, Venezuela)

Mad River Mountain Biking, Rt. 17, Waitsfield, VT 05673; phone: (800) 777-4933

Metro Pacific Tours, Inc., Box 230973, Tigard, OR 97223; phone: (503) 620-8115 (California, Oregon, Washington)

Michigan Bicycle Touring, 3512 Red School Rd., Kingsley, MI 49649; phone: (616) 263-5885 (Michigan)

Mississippi River Bicycle Tours, Rt. 2, Box 299, Greenville, IL 62246; phone: (618) 664-1776 (Illinois, Kentucky, Louisiana, Mississippi, Missouri, Tennessee)

Missouri Meanders, 5157 Green Trace Ln., St. Louis, MO 63128; phone: (314) 849-4326.(Illinois, Missouri, Texas, Wisconsin)

Mountain Bike School & Touring Center, Mount Snow Resort, Mount Snow, VT 05356; phone: (802) 464-3333 (Vermont)

Mountain Bike Specialists, 340 S. Camino Del Rio, Durango, CO 81301; phone: (303) 247-4066 (Colorado)

New England Bicycle Tours, Box D, Randolph, VT 05060; phone: (802) 728-3261

New Zealand Pedaltours, 522 29th Ave., South Seattle, WA 98144; phone: (206) 323-2080 (New Zealand)

Nichols Expeditions, 497 N. Main, Moab, UT 84532; phone: (800) 635-1792 (Arizona, Idaho, Utah) ·

Northstar Bicycle Tours, 113 Crawley Ave., Pennington, NJ 08534; phone: (609) 737-8346 (New Jersey, Virginia)

Northwest Bicycle Touring Society, 6166 92nd Ave. SE, Mercer Island, WA 98040; phone: (206) 232-2694

Northwest Passage, 1130 Greenleaf Ave., Wilmette, IL 60091; phone: (708) 256-4409

Northwest Touring Adventures, 8908 S.W. Cemetery Rd., Vashon, WA 98070; phone: (206) 463-2539 (Oregon, Washington; British Columbia)

Ocean Island Bike Tours, Box 34, Laie, HI 96762; phone: (808) 293-5296 (Hawaii)

Odyssey Adventures & Blue Marble Travel, Baxter Place, Suite 505, Portland, ME 04101; phone: (800) 544-3216 (Montana, Wyoming; Austria, Denmark, France, Germany, Italy, Portugal, Spain, Switzerland)

Okanagan Bike Roads Cycle Tours, 2-516 Papineau St., Pentiction British Columbia, Canada V2A 4X6; phone: (604) 493-BIKE

On the Loose Bicycle Vacations, 1030 Merced St., Berkeley, CA 94707; phone: (800) 346-6712

Oregon Cycling Adventures, 1324 NW Vicksburg Bend, OR 97701; phone: (503) 388-0064 (Arizona, Oregon; Canada)

Otter Bar Lodge, Box 210, Forks of Salmon, CA 96031; phone: (916) 462-4772 (northern California)

Outback with Bodfish, Box 69, Chester, CA 96020; phone: (916) 258-4296

Outer Edge Expeditions, 45500 Pontiac Trail, Suite E, Walled Lake, MI 48390; phone: (800) 332-5235 (Amazon Jungle, Australia, Canada, Indonesia, Irian Jaya, New Zealand, Peru)

Outward Bound Hurricane Island, Box 429, Rockland, ME 04841; phone: (800) 341-1744 (Maine, New Hampshire, Vermont; continental United States; Quebec)

Pacific-Atlantic Cycling (PAC) Tour, Box 73, Harvard, IL 60033; phone: (815) 943-3171 (Rocky Mountains, transcontinental United States)

Paradise Bicycle Tours, Inc., Box 1726, Evergreen, CO 80439; phone: (303) 670-1842 (Belize, Central America, East Africa, Kenya, New Zealand)

Paradise Pedallers, Box 34625, Charlotte, NC 28324; phone: (704) 335-8687 (North Carolina; Australia, New Zealand)

Pedal for Power, Box 898-T, Atkinson, NH 03811; phone: (800) 762-BIKE (transcontinental United States, California to Massachusetts and Maine to Florida)

Pedal the Peaks, 2878 W. Long Circle #H, Littleton, CO 80120

Pedal the Peaks of Northern Vermont, Box 93, Main St., Montgomery Center, VT 05471; phone: (800) 882-7460 (Vermont)

Peter Costello, Ltd., Box 23490, Baltimore, MD 21203; phone: (301) 783-1229 (Scotland)

Pocono Whitewater, Ltd., H.C.2, Box 2245, Jim Thorpe, PA 18229; phone: (717) 325-3656

Progressive Travels, Luxury Bicycling, 1932 1st Ave., Suite 1100, Seattle, WA 98101; phone: (800) 245-2229 (Mississippi, Washington; Africa, Bahamas, Belize, France, Holland, Italy, New Zealand)

Randonnee Tours Ltd., 101-191 River Ave., Winnipeg, Manitoba, Canada R3G 2J7; phone: (204) 475-6939 (France)

Red Roads Cycle Tours, Ltd., Box 2533, Charlottetown, Prince Edward Island, Canada C1A 8C2; phone: (902) 628-6218 (Prince Edward Island)

REI Adventures, Box 1938, Sumner, WA 98390; phone: (800) 622-2236 (continental United States, Alaska; Central America, China, eastern Europe, Nepal, the Pacific, South America)

Rent-A-Bike, Box 1204, Station B, Ottawa, Ontario, Canada K1P 5R3; phone: (613) 233-0268

Rim Tours, 94 W. 100 S, Moab, UT 84532; phone: (800) 626-7335 (Colorado, Utah)

Roads Less Traveled, Box 8187, Longmont, CO 80501; phone: (303) 678-8750 (Colorado, New Mexico, South Dakota, Utah)

Rocky Mountain Cycle Tours, Box 1978, Canmore, Alberta, Canada T0L 0M0; phone: (403) 678-6770 (western Canada; Hawaii; France, Germany, Italy, Switzerland)

Royal Bike Tours, RR 1, Box 1890, Lopez Island, WA 98261; phone: (800) 522-BIKE (San Juan Islands, Washington; Scotland)

Rusland International, Box 7915, Tacoma, WA 98407; phone: (206) 759-7547 (Russia)

Safaricentre, 3201 N. Sepulveda Blvd., Manhattan Beach, CA 90266; phone: (800) 223-6046

St. Louis Bicycle Touring Society, 11816 St. Charles Rock Rd., Bridgeton, MO 63044; phone: (314) 739-5180 (Colorado, Illinois, Missouri, Montana, Utah, Wisconsin; France, Germany, Ireland, New Zealand)

San Juan Hut Systems, Box 1663, Telluride, CO 81435; phone: (303) 728-6935 (Colorado, Utah)

Sea to Sky Cycling, Box 1523, Whistler, British Columbia, Canada V0N 1B0; phone: (604) 938-1233 (British Columbia)

Sense Adventures, Box 216, Kingston 7, Jamaica; phone: (809) 927-2097

Serenity Unlimited, Inc., 2 Lake St., Monroe, NY 10950; phone: (914) 782-7145 (Vermont)

Sierra Club, 730 Polk St., San Francisco, CA 94109; phone: (415) 923-5630

Singles Bicycle Tours, Inc., 550 First St., Collingwood, Ontario, Canada L9Y 1C1 (Canada)

Ski Sawmill Bike Center, RR 1, Box 5, Rt. 287, Morris, PA 16938; phone: (717) 533-7542 (Pennsylvania)

Southwest Cycle Expeditions, Box 30731, Flagstaff, AZ 86003; phone: (602) 526-4882 (Arizona, Colorado, Utah)

Spinning Spokes, 8244 S.W. 184th Terr., Miami, FL 33157; phone: (305) 233-2135

Spinning Wheel Bicycle Tours, Box 51, Jordan Station, Ontario, Canada L0R 1S0; phone: (416) 562-7169

Student Hosteling Program, Ashfield Rd., Conway, MA 01341; phone: (413) 369-4275 (California, Maine, Massachusetts, New Hampshire, Oregon, Vermont, Washington, Wyoming; transcontinental United States; Canadian Rockies; Europe)

Sunny Land Tours, 166 Main St., Hackensack, NJ 07601; phone: (201) 487-2150 (Austria, Czechoslovakia, Hungary, Poland, Russia)

Sunset Bicycle Tours, Inc., 455 University Ave., Charlottetown, Prince Edward Island, Canada C1A 8C2; phone: (902) 892-0606

Sunshine Bicycle Tours, 3435 Johnson St., Hollywood, FL 33021; phone: (305) 966-8666 (Florida Keys; Bahamas)

Suwannee Bicycle Association, Box 247, White Springs, FL 32097; phone: (904) 878-2042 (Florida; Australia, New Zealand, Yucatan)

Tandem Touring Co., 3131 Endicott, Boulder, CO 80303; phone: (303) 499-3178 (California, Colorado; France)

Texas Bicycle Tours, Box 740981, Houston, TX 77274; phone: (713) 771-8004

Timberline Bicycle Tours, 7975 E. Harvard #J, Denver, CO 80231; phone: (303) 759-3804 (California, Michigan, Minnesota, Wisconsin, Pacific Northwest; United States National Parks)

Timeless Cycles, Box 18324, Boulder, CO 80308; phone: (303) 499-8965 (England, Scandinavia)

Tour de Caña, Box 7293, Philadelphia, PA 19101; phone: (215) 222-1253

Tour de Cape, Box 1259, Marshfield, MA 02050

Touring Exchange, Box 265, Port Townsend, WA 98368; phone: (206) 385-0667 (Belize, Costa Rica, Mexico)

Trailside Lodge, HCR #65, Coffee House Rd., Killington, VT 05751; phone: (802) 422-3532 (Vermont)

Travel-Lyn, Inc., Box 9035, Missoula, MT 59807; phone: (406) 728-5223 (Europe)

Travent International, Box 305, Waterbury Center, VT 05677; phone: (800) 325-3009 (western Europe)

Triskell Cycle Tours, 33 Langland Dr., Northway, Sedgley DY3 3TH, England

True Wheel Tours, 3 E. Woolerton St., Delhi, NY 13753; phone: (607) 746-2737 (New York; Europe, Jamaica)

Two Wheel Tours, Box 2655, Littleton, CO 80161; phone: (303) 798-4601

Two Wheel Tours International, Box 1235, Bloomington, IN 47402; phone: (812) 336-1214

Ultimate Country Cycling Tours, 30 Cedar Ave., Pointe Claire, Quebec, Canada H9S 4Y1; phone: (514) 697-9496

Urban Trails, 30 Norwood Ave., Staten Island, NY 10304

Utah Mountain Biking Tours, 942 E. 7145 S, Suite A-202, Midvale, UT 84047

Van Gogh Bicycle Tours, Box 57, Winchester, MA 01890; phone: (617) 721-0850 (Netherlands)

VCC Four Seasons Cycling, Box 145, Waterbury Center, VT 05677; phone: (802) 244-5135 (Connecticut, Florida, Hawaii, Kentucky, Maine, Maryland, Massachusetts, Mississippi, New York, North Carolina, Pennsylvania, South Carolina, Vermont, Virginia, West Virginia; Nova Scotia, Ontario, Prince Edward Island)

Vermont Bicycle Touring, Box 711, Bristol, VT 05443; phone: (802) 453-4811 (Hawaii, Maine, Pennsylvania, Vermont, Virginia; Nova Scotia, England, France, Holland, Ireland, Italy, New Zealand)

Vermont Mountain Bike Tours, Box 685, Pittsfield, VT 05762; phone: (802) 746-8580 (Vermont)

Victor Vincente of America, 1582 Pride St., Simi Valley, CA 93065; phone: (805) 527-1991 (southern California)

The Villages at Killington, Killington, VT 05751

Wandering Wheels, Inc., Box 207, Upland, IN 46989; phone: (317) 998-7490 (Arizona, California, Florida, Maine, New Hampshire, Vermont; transcontinental United States)

Western Spirit Cycling, Box 411, Moab, UT 84532; phone: (800) 845-BIKE (Colorado, Idaho, Utah)

West Virginia Bike Tours, Box 143, Buchannon, WV 26201; phone: (304) 472-6409 (West Virginia)

Wild Onion Tours, Box 257781, Chicago, IL 60625; phone: (312) 275-BIKE (Illinois, Indiana, Michigan, Wisconsin)

Wine Country Bike Tours, 1200 Halyard Dr., Santa Rosa, CA 95041; phone: (800) 368-6771 (California)

Womantrek, Box 20643, Seattle, WA 98102; phone: (800) 477-TREK

Woodswomen, Inc., 25 W. Diamond Lake Rd., Minneapolis, MN 55419; phone: (612) 822-3809 (California; midwestern United States; France, Ireland, New Zealand)

World Expeditions, 78 George St., Ottawa, Ontario, Canada K1N 5W1; phone: (613) 230-8676 (China, Europe)

World Travelers, Inc., 6612 S.E. 24th St., Mercer Island, WA 98040; phone: (800) 426-3610 (Austria, England, France, Germany, Italy, Spain)

Zahn's Glacier Tours, Box 75, Jennison Rd., Milford, NH 03055; phone: (603) 673-1908 (Austria, Bavaria, Dolomites)

CREDITS

The information in this book is drawn from these and other articles in *Bicycling* magazine.

"Cycling's Newest Industry" David Coburn, "Cycling's Newest Industry," March 1991.

"How to Shop for a Tour" Nelson Pena, "How to Shop for a Tour," March 1991.

"Luxury Tours" Joe Kita, "Luxury Tours," February 1989.

"Bed-and-Breakfast (and Bike)" Joe Kita, "Bed & Breakfast & Bike," June 1990.

"Cycling the Ski Resorts" Tim Blumenthal, "Cycling the Ski Resorts," August 1991.

"A Ride of Passage" David M. Abramson, "A Ride of Passage," April 1988.

"Planning Your Journey" Gary D. MacFadden, "Planning Your Passage," April 1988.

"Factor In the Prevailing Winds" Tim and Jennifer Klingler, "Winds of Change," April 1988.

"Cameras and Diaries to Record the Memories" Byron Reed, Alys Culhane, "Photographs and Memories," April 1988.

"What to Pack" *Bicycling* editors, "You Can Take It With You," April 1988.

"Every Cyclist's Dream" Joe Kita, "Every Cyclist's Dream," May 1990.

"Bicycling in the New Europe" Larry Kilman, "The New Europe," May 1990.

"Euro Tour Planner" Liz Smutko, "Euro Tour Planner," May 1990.

"Mountain Bike Heaven" Nelson Pena, "C'est Super!" May 1990.

"When You Fly and Your Bike Flies with You" Liz Smutko, "Flight Lessons," May 1990.

"Boxing a Bike for Shipment" Jim Langley, "Boxing a Bike," September/October 1991.

"Handling a Heavily Loaded Bike" Geoff Drake, "Loaded Touring," June 1991.

"High Mileage without Discomfort" Connie Carpenter Phinney, "Long-Distance Comfort," August 1988.

"Safe Cycling in Wet Weather" Geoff Drake, "Riding in the Rain," April 1991.

"High-Altitude Cycling" Scott Martin, "Riding High," August 1991.

"A Guide to Bike Tour Companies" editors of *Bicycling,* "Adventure Touring Guide," March 1993.

Photographs

Pages 84–89: Mel Lindstrom
Page 92: John Hamel

Illustrations

Page 50: Map by Scott A. MacNeil
Page 104: *Bicycling Plus Mountain Bike,* August 1991